OLD TESTAMENT STUDIES

Edited by

David J. Reimer

OLD TESTAMENT STUDIES

The mid-twentieth century was a period of great confidence in the study of the Hebrew Bible: many historical and literary questions appeared to be settled, and a constructive theological programme was well under-way. Now, at the turn of the century, the picture is very different. Conflicting positions are taken on historical issues; scholars disagree not only on how to pose the questions, but also on what to admit as evidence. Sharply divergent methods are used in ever more popular literary studies of the Bible. Theological ferment persists, but is the Bible's theological vision coherent, or otherwise?

The Old Testament Studies series provides an outlet for thoughtful debate in the fundamental areas of biblical history, theology, and literature. Any biblical theology must soon grapple with the central notion of 'covenant'. In this volume, Professor Rendtorff examines expressions of covenant language, illuminating the way in which ancient Israel's thinking about the relationship between God and community developed over time.

THE COVENANT FORMULA

THE COVENANT FORMULA

An Exegetical and Theological Investigation

Rolf Rendtorff

Translated by
Margaret Kohl

T&T CLARK
EDINBURGH

T&T CLARK LTD
59 GEORGE STREET
EDINBURGH EH2 2LQ
SCOTLAND

Copyright © T&T Clark Ltd, 1998

Authorised English translation of *Die Bundesformel* © Verlag Katholisches
Bibelwerk, Stuttgart, 1995

First published 1998

ISBN 0 567 08605 4

British Library Cataloguing-in-Publication Data
A catalogue record for this book is available from the British Library

Typeset by Fakenham Photosetting Limited
Printed and bound in Great Britain by Bookcraft Ltd, Avon

CONTENTS

PREFACE

This study has arisen out of work on a theology of the Old Testament. In examining the assembly of themes which is summed up under the catchword 'covenant', I became aware that one essential element in this great and complex field has still, up to now, been little investigated: the element known as 'the covenant formula'. This expression is used for the declaration: 'I will be your God, you shall be my people', a pronouncement which we encounter more than thirty times in various books of the Hebrew Bible. It is formula-like in its essential elements, even though in individual cases we find a number of variants. Rudolf Smend devoted a brief study to it more than thirty years ago, and this has been frequently cited ever since. But we still lack further studies which investigate more precisely the use of this formula in the different textual sectors, and also, and especially, its theological usage. Another question is important here too: how is the covenant formula related to other 'set' or established elements, above all the terms 'covenant' and 'choose'? And how far does it belong together with these within a wider theological complex?

The following exposition indicates the path which I myself have taken in my investigations. After some preliminary considerations of method (Chapter I), I have begun with an exegetical examination of each individual passage in which we encounter the covenant formula (Chapter II); here I have followed the order of the biblical books. After that, I have extended the study beyond the individual texts, enquiring under various aspects about the relation of the covenant formula to its respective contexts (Chapter III). As a final step, I have tried to order and sum up theologically the results arrived at (Chapter IV). In this process, I have continually viewed the individual texts from shifting standpoints, while attempting to avoid unnecessary repetition. Explicit cross-references in the notes to earlier or later passages in the book have been reduced to a minimum, and I would ask readers to draw on the Contents and the Indexes.

Norbert Lohfink encouraged me to put forward my observations in a separate publication. Erich Zenger was immediately willing to include this little study in the Stuttgarter Bibelstudien. I should like to express my sincere thanks to both of them.

Rolf Rendtorff

TRANSLATOR'S NOTE

Biblical quotations have been taken from the New Revised Standard Version, but changes of wording have often been required in order to reflect the nuances of the German text. Verse numbers follow the numbering in the Hebrew Bible. Where the English Bible differs, the English verse number has been added in angle brackets.

Articles are cited in the notes with reference to the publication in which they are probably most readily available. Full bibliographical details, with the date of the original publication in each case, may be found in the Bibliography.

I should like to thank Professor Rendtorff for his great help in the preparation of the translation.

Margaret Kohl

ABBREVIATIONS

AnBib	Analecta biblica, Rome
AThANT	Abhandlungen zur Theologie des Alten und Neuen Testaments, Zurich
BEThL	Bibliotheca ephemeridum theologicarum lovaniensium, Gembloux
BEvTh	Beiträge zur Evangelischen Theologie, Munich
BHTh	Beiträge zur historischen Theologie, Tübingen
BK	Biblischer Kommentar, Neukirchen-Vluyn
BWANT	Beiträge zur Wissenschaft vom Alten und Neuen Testament, Leipzig
BZAW	Beihefte zur Zeitschrift für die alttestamentliche Wissenschaft, Berlin and New York
BZ NF	*Biblische Zeitschrift, Neue Folge*, Freiburg
CB.OT	Coniectanea biblica, Old Testament series, Stockholm
ET	English translation
FRLANT	Forschungen zur Religion und Literatur des Alten und Neuen Testaments, Göttingen
GAT	Grundrisse zum Alten Testament, Göttingen
HAT	Handbuch zum Alten Testament, Tübingen
JBL	*Journal of Biblical Literature*, Atlanta
JBT	*Jahrbuch für biblische Theologie*, Neukirchen-Vluyn
KAT	Kommentar zum Alten Testament, Gütersloh
OBO	Orbis biblicus et orientalis, Göttingen
QD	Questiones Disputatae, Freiburg
SKG:G	Schriften der Königsberger Gelehrten Gesellschaft: Geisteswissenschaftliche Klasse, Halle and Saale
TB	Theologische Bücherei, Munich
TDOT	Theological Dictionary of the Old Testament (translation of ThWAT; in progress), Grand Rapids
ThSt(B)	Theologische Studien, Zurich
ThWAT	Theologisches Wörterbuch zum Alten Testament, Stuttgart
ThZ	*Theologische Zeitschrift*, Basel
VT	*Vetus Testamentum*, Leiden
WMANT	Wissenschaftliche Monographien zum Alten und Neuen Testament, Neukirchen-Vluyn

ZAW   *Zeitschrift für die alttestamentliche Wissenschaft*, Berlin
ZKTh   *Zeitschrift für Katholische Theologie*, Innsbruck

INTRODUCTION

The Opening

You are the LORD, you alone;
you have made heaven,
the heaven of heavens, with all their host,
the earth and all that is on it,
the seas and all that is in them.
To all of them you give life,
and the host of heaven worships you.
You are the LORD,
the God who chose Abram
and brought him out of Ur of the Chaldeans
and gave him the name Abraham,
and you found his heart faithful before you,
and made with him a covenant
to give to his descendants the land of the Canaanite, the Hittite,
the Amorite, the Perizzite, the Jebusite, and the Girgashite;
and you have fulfilled your promise,
for you are righteous.

(Neh. 9.6–8)

This is the way the great prayer begins in the service of repentance which in the book of Ezra-Nehemiah follows Ezra's reading of the Torah and the subsequent Feast of Booths. This prayer is remarkable in many ways, not least in what it says about Abraham.

The first significant thing is that Abraham's election is named as the first event after the creation. If we note the structure of the text, we can even say that this divine act is seen on almost the same level as creation itself. Both are introduced with the emphatic אַתָּה־הוּא יהוה, 'You yourself are Yhwh', which does not occur again as an introductory formula anywhere else in this prayer. The whole passage which embraces these two events is then concluded with the solemn formula כִּי צַדִּיק אַתָּה, 'for you are righteous'. This formula is found again only once, in slightly varied form, right at the end of the prayer, in the description of the people's present distress, where it stresses that God has fulfilled his obligations towards Israel, and that the misery which Israel is suffering is the consequence of the guilt of its responsible leaders (v. 33). So by way of this concluding formula too, the special position of what God has done for Abraham is once again stressed.

The first statement is that God has 'chosen' Abraham. The verb used

1

here, בָּחַר, is pre-eminently a set term in the theological language of Deuteronomy. But there it is applied to Israel as a whole, whereas its explicit application to Abraham is special to Nehemiah 9. The following statements show that the author of this prayer is familiar with the traditions as we find them in the book of Genesis. The choosing of Abraham manifested itself in concrete form when God brought him out of 'Ur in Chaldea', a declaration which is a word-for-word echo of Gen. 15.7. Abram is renamed Abraham in the great divine speech in Genesis . 17 (v. 5). When the prayer says that God has found Abraham's heart נֶאֱמָן, 'faithful' or 'reliable', this again echoes Genesis 15, where v. 6 uses the word וְהֶאֱמִן, 'and he believed', which is closely related in Hebrew. The passage then goes on to say that God has made a בְּרִית, a 'covenant', with Abraham. Genesis 15 and Genesis 17 talk about this, the wording in Neh. 9.8 being closer to that of Gen. 15.18–21. There the making of the covenant is expressed by the technical term כָּרַת, which can also mean 'cut', and is frequently used for the conclusion of a covenant. The fact that the land is promised to Abraham's 'seed', that is to say his descendants, also accords with Gen. 15.18. Finally, as in Gen. 15.19–21, a list of tribes still living in the country follows, although in Neh. 9.8 this is shorter and names the peoples in a different order.[1]

This last observation shows that the author of Nehemiah 9 did not simply 'copy down' the already existing Genesis text. But he was familiar with the traditions related there—and apparently already in their present arrangement. In the light of their language and their theological context, there can hardly be any doubt that Genesis 15 and Genesis 17 represent different spheres of tradition;[2] but for the author of Nehemiah 9 they evidently already belonged together. Moreover he uses the verb בחר for God's act in choosing Abraham, a word which does not occur with this meaning in the book of Genesis, but which belongs to the language of Deuteronomy. In this instance he extended the tradition independently, for it is only here that this expression is used in connection with Abraham.

[1] L. Gaston, 'Abraham and the Righteousness of God', in *Paul and the Torah* (1987), 53f., understands the statement about Abraham's 'being faithful' (אמן Niphal) as parallel to Gen. 15.16: Abraham 'believed' (אמן Hiphil). That passage goes on: 'and he reckoned it to him as righteousness', the subject of the second clause not thereby being named. In Neh. 9.8, however, the clause that follows runs: 'for you [God] are righteous', thus making it unequivocally God who is termed righteous. Gaston sees this as evidence that Genesis 15 is also talking about God's righteousness, not Abraham's. This view had already been maintained in the thirteenth century by Nachmanides. (Cf. also M. Oeming, 'Ist Gen 15,6 ein Beleg für die Anrechnung des Glaubens zur Gerechtigkeit?', ZAW 95 (1983), 182–197; R. Mosis, '"Glauben" und "Gerechtigkeit"—zu Gen 15,6', in *Die Väter Israels: Festschrift J. Schreiner* (1989), 225–275; and D. U. Rotzoll, 'Gen 15,16—ein Beleg für den Glauben als Werkgerechtigkeit', ZAW 106 (1994), 21–27.)

[2] Genesis 17 is an important representative of the Pentateuch's 'Priestly' stratum of composition, whereas Genesis 15 must be assigned to the 'Deuteronomistic' stratum; cf. E. Blum, *Studien zur Komposition des Pentateuch* (1984), 362ff.

This first brief glance at a 'late' text of the Hebrew Bible is designed
to show first of all how traditions are linked here which are generally
treated separately in modern Old Testament scholarship. In research,
'covenant' and 'election' are presented as two quite different subjects,
so that there are hardly any connecting lines between the investigations
into the one or the other theme. Yet we have seen how close the links
between these themes are in Nehemiah 9. If from this point we turn back
to the 'older' traditions, a number of relationships already emerge there
too. This becomes even clearer if we expand the terminological field
further, and include the so-called 'covenant formula'. This expression is
largely used as term for the phrase 'I will be your God and you shall be
my people', with its variants. Again, studies of this formula are largely
independent of studies of the two subjects already mentioned. This is
particularly striking because here the connections immediately leap to
the eye. To mention only two examples: (1) In Gen. 17.7 the initial
purpose of the covenant which God 'establishes' with Abraham and his
descendants is 'in order to be God for you and for your descendants
after you': this reason is given first place. Here 'covenant' and
'covenant formula' cannot be separated. (2) The same is true of the
word בחר, 'choose', which in Deuteronomy has entered into close
association with the covenant formula. Deut. 7.6 and 14.2 run, in almost
identical terms, 'For you are a people holy to Yhwh your God (and)
Yhwh (your God) has chosen you to be a people for his own possession,
out of all the peoples that are on the face of the earth.' Here, therefore,
the covenant formula and the pronouncement of election cannot be
separated.

Finally, however, we must go yet one step further. The fixation on
particular terms often leads to a narrowing down of the enquiry. Again
an example: in the first divine speech on Sinai, in Ex. 19.5f., we find
typical elements of Deuteronomic election theology: 'You shall be my
possession before all peoples'. But the word 'choose' is missing. An
examination concentrated on terms will include at best a marginal
consideration of this text. For the covenant formula too this text will be
marginal, because although it contains the word סְגֻלָּה, 'possession',
which is typical for Deuteronomy, it does not use the word in
connection with the word 'people'.[3] Finally, the text also includes the
word ברית, 'covenant', but it is used in a somewhat untypical way. This
central Pentateuchal text is thus often marginalized in investigations.
But in the context of our present enquiry it shows very clearly that
theological ideas did not by any means always crystallise into particular
terms, as it were, but that the terms often only cover a partial aspect of
what is meant and said; and, moreover, that these terms are by no means

---

[3] R. Smend, 'Die Bundesformel', *ThSt(B)* 68 (1963), 13, calls Ex. 19.5 'a softened
form'.

always used where today's reader would expect them. This is also true
ultimately speaking (to take a further example) of the idea of Abraham's
election. For the ingenuous reader of the Bible, it seems self-evident that
God 'chose' Abraham, and that with this act God's history of election in
general began. But in God's first address to Abraham in Gen. 12.1–3, no
corresponding term is in fact used, and the technical Old Testament term
בחר, 'choose', is, as we have seen, applied to Abraham for the first time
in Nehemiah 9.

I

SOME PRELIMINARY CONSIDERATIONS OF METHOD

1. *Historical Criticism*

The preceding brief introduction implied criticism of certain aspects of research as it has been carried out hitherto. I must here develop and justify this a little further. In so doing, I should like to say first that the methodological approaches which I shall be discussing grew up out of their own respective periods, and had their justification, and largely speaking their importance too, in their own particular contexts. If today I am to some degree calling them in question, that is mainly because in my view the study of the Hebrew Bible is still on the move hermeneutically and theologically, and has consequently raised new questions. To some extent this goes hand in hand with new insights into the historical ordering of the biblical traditions which have also made necessary the revision of certain earlier views.[1]

Let me begin with a quite fundamental question: what is the real object of the interpretation of the Hebrew Bible? To reduce this question to a highly simplified pair of alternatives: Is our object *the history* which lies behind the texts—the history which we are trying to explore as thoroughly as possible? Or is it *the texts* themselves, whose utterances we are trying to grasp and understand? Ever since the last century, a method of study based on 'historical criticism' has dominated Old Testament scholarship. Drawing on differences of style and viewpoint, as well as on unevennesses and disunities in the text, the exponents of this method try to detect and elicit earlier strata or sources of the text as we have it today. This has led to a way of looking at the texts which is essentially diachronic—that is to say, to a pre-eminent concern with the earlier stages of the now-extant text—as far as possible with the oldest, 'original' text in each case. The textual strata which are assumed to be later are considered too, but in such a way that there is a clear gradation: what is older deserves more attention, and is often also viewed as more valuable, because it is in a number of ways 'more original', whereas—according to this viewpoint—in the later stages of the text's history, traditions were frequently reinterpreted, and were often not even properly understood. In addition, the later periods are often viewed as times of decline and disintegration. In all this the text in its present, final form hardly comes into view at all.

---

[1] Cf. here R. Rendtorff, 'The Paradigm is Changing: Hopes—and Fears', *Biblical Interpretation* 1 (1993), 34–53.

This diachronic way of looking at the texts goes hand in hand with a dominant concern about the history that lies behind the texts. The individual textual stages are viewed as witnesses to particular epochs in history and the history of religion, so that the interpretation of the text ministers for a great part to the reconstruction of the history of Israel's religion. It must, however, be said that this reconstruction is to a very large extent dependent on the presumed dating of the text's different strata, as well as on related assumptions about the historical reliability of what is reported. In recent years and decades profound changes have emerged, or have been heralded, with regard to both these aspects.

Let us make this clear to ourselves from the example of Abraham. The question about the 'historical' Abraham is now completely dismissed by some scholars,[2] whereas others view the traditions about Abraham or the patriarchs as traditions about the early period of Israel's history which are valuable and have to be taken seriously, even though there are wide differences in detail among proponents of this school of thought.[3] The evaluation of this question means that the possibility of using the texts about Abraham for the reconstruction of Israel's early history (especially its social history and the history of its religion) is judged in highly divergent ways. It is true that hardly anyone today would attempt to interpret the texts available to us in Genesis 12–25 as direct accounts of the life of the historical Abraham, and as a literal reproduction of what he thought and said. But these chapters are often viewed as an important source for Israel's early social and religious history, and utilised accordingly. If, on the other hand, Abraham's historicity is called into question altogether, the possibility of any such assessment falls to the ground simply of its own accord.

This question is closely linked with the question about the dating of the texts. According to the 'classic' and still largely prevailing view, the oldest source of the Pentateuch, the so-called Yahwist, dates from the early years of the monarchy, i.e. from about the ninth century (or from even earlier, the tenth century, the age of Solomon, or perhaps from the eighth century, before the destruction of the Northern Kingdom in 722). In addition, it contains traditions which reach back into the period before the formation of the state, i.e. to before *c*.1000 BC. This means that a diachronic study by way of these texts can penetrate far back into the early history of Israel. A more recent position, on the other hand, dates 'the Yahwist' (and hence the beginnings of the Pentateuch in its

---

[2] See, e.g., T. L. Thompson, *The Historicity of the Patriarchal Narratives: The Quest for the Historical Abraham* (1974); J. Van Seters, *Abraham in History and Tradition* (1975).

[3] E.g. C. Westermann, *Genesis 12–36* (ET 1985); H. Donner, *Geschichte des Volkes Israel und seiner Nachbarn*, vol. 1 (1984); R. Albertz, *A History of Israelite Religion in the Old Testament Period* (ET 1994). For an extremely conservative view see A. R. Millard, 'Abraham', *Anchor Bible Dictionary*, vol. 1 (1992), 35–41.

literary form) only to the period of the Babylonian exile, i.e. brings these beginnings forward to the sixth century.[4] In this case the figure of Abraham must be judged in a completely different way. It is understood essentially as a cast back to Israel's earlier salvation-history traditions, springing from the era of collapse and reconstruction.

My purpose in saying this is to show how much an interpretation orientated towards a history behind the texts is dependent on particular preliminary decisions which are reached only partly in the context of the texts themselves, and in most cases are not directly arrived at through the interpretation of these texts. This means that in the interpretation the possibility or impossibility of particular questions is also largely predetermined. For example, is there any point in asking: 'Did God make a covenant with Abraham?' Or—if we prefer to formulate the question from a human standpoint—'Did Abraham believe that he stood in a covenant with God?' If we support an early date for 'the Yahwist', and a still earlier date for the traditions he took over, we can take up this question as a useful one in the framework of reflections about 'the religion of the patriarchs', even if here Abraham may appear less as an individual figure than as the representative of Israel's early history and religion, before the formation of the state. But if the text is dated much later, the question alters fundamentally. It can then only be: what was the idea of God's covenant with Abraham supposed to express at the time when the texts came into being (which again is only a matter of conjecture)?

In all these questions, the biblical texts are *material* for questions and problems which do not emerge from the texts themselves, or at least not directly. But if we ask: what do the texts say about God's covenant with Abraham?, a great deal alters. This question too can be put diachronically: what do the various textual strata have to say about God's covenant with Abraham—what does 'the Yahwist' say, or 'the Priestly Writing', and so forth? In this case too the question is really directed to the history lying behind the texts, because hypothetically deduced figures (e.g. the Yahwist) are interrogated about their views, and the answers are then written into the equally hypothetically deduced period of the figures in question. But just how uncertain the results are is shown precisely by the discussion which I have already described about the dating of the Yahwist.

The question about what the texts are saying can also be put synchronically, however: what does the text say in the form in which we now have it? The reading of the text in its given continuity which follows from this question leads us simply of itself to see God's

---

[4] If calculations do not reckon with the existence of a Yahwist 'source' (as, e.g., in E. Blum, *Die Komposition der Vätergeschichte* (1984) and *Studien zur Komposition des Pentateuch* (1990), the questions take a somewhat different form; but the result is not an early date for the older strata of the Pentateuch.

covenant with Abraham in the context of God's covenant with Noah, which preceded it, and God's covenant with Israel on Sinai, which followed.[5] And this also raises the question: are there different covenants or *a single* covenant? (The Hebrew Bible knows the word ברית, covenant, only in the singular!) And how are the different forms the covenant takes related to one another? The synchronic standpoint by no means excludes recognition of the differences in language and style which are the outcome of the fusing of different strata and elements of tradition in the final text as we have it. The literary-critical approach started from entirely justifiable observations about the differences between the strata of tradition which were termed 'sources'; and these observations, which were continually subjected to critical reflection, contributed in many cases to a better and more differentiated understanding of the text. The mistake—as we see it in retrospect today— was (and often still is) that the primary exegetical task is seen to be as follows: to isolate the different presumed strata of tradition from each other, to 'reconstruct' each of them (although they still, after all, remain no more than hypotheses, conjectures!) and then to construe them, each for itself, instead of reading them and interpreting them in the context in which they are now given to us. But the Bible as it has come down to us actually came into being through the fusing of these different elements of tradition, and we are undoubtedly supposed to read and interpret it in this present form. The exegetical task is therefore to understand and interpret the text in the shape in which we now have it, in its final 'canonical' form.

Form Criticism

As well as the viewpoint based on historical criticism, we must mention still another methodological approach, which has also become of great importance for our subject: form criticism. Here, in my view, it is very much more true to say that this method has contributed to a better and more differentiated understanding of the Old Testament texts. The recognition of the literary structures of the texts, the definition of genres arrived at through the comparison of different passages, and finally the question about their *Sitz im Leben*—their setting in life—have greatly promoted insights into the history of Biblical literature and the location of that literature in Israel's social and religious life.[6]

---

[5] This, for example, does away with the question as to why the Priestly Writing shows no knowledge of a covenant on Sinai (thus W. Zimmerli, 'Sinaibund und Abrahambund: Ein Beitrag zum Verständnis der Priesterschrift', *ThZ* 16 (1960), 268–280); for the Priestly texts are one component of the great complex in which the covenant on Sinai plays a central part.

[6] Cf. K. Koch, *The Growth of the Biblical Tradition: The Form-Critical Method* (ET 1969); R. Rendtorff, *The Old Testament: An Introduction* (ET 1985), 77–128.

Here too, however, form criticism proves to have a marked tendency to isolate individual, often very small textual fragments, over against their context. Hermann Gunkel, the founder of form criticism, talked about 'smallest literary units', which had to be worked out in detail and defined. In this process, larger textual complexes hardly came into view. In the case of the subject that concerns us here, interest was directed primarily towards set phraseology, 'formulas' and 'formularies', and their *Sitz im Leben*. Here, as far as 'the covenant' is concerned, the discovery of comparable formula-like elements and cultic covenantal ceremonies in other ancient oriental cultures was of great interest, and led to detailed investigations and discussions of the rituals and rites attending the conclusion of covenants, discussions in which the Old Testament texts in their present contexts hardly played an independent role at all.[7]

It was precisely this way of looking at things which led to the practice of treating the themes 'covenant' and 'election', as well as 'covenant formula', in almost complete isolation from one another in Old Testament research, on the basis of their formula-like usage in each given case. Here, moreover, form criticism went hand in hand with a viewpoint wholly orientated towards concepts and terms, a *Begriffs-geschichte* ('concept history') which concentrated on particular Hebrew termini—above all ברית, 'covenant', and בחר, 'choose', as well as on the formal structure of the two pronouncements (or double pronounce-ment) 'to be God for you—to be a people for me'. Thus in more recent Old Testament literature we have the impression that 'covenant', 'election' and 'covenant formula' are three completely different themes.[8]

This impression is closely connected with what was said earlier in this chapter. With respect to each of these three sectors, scholars enquire about the earliest, 'original' state of things, so that 'later' developments in the text hardly enter their orbit. The text in Nehemiah 9, which was our starting point, is a highly characteristic example of a late text of this kind which has received hardly any attention.[9] But it is just such a text which shows how these themes were thought together in Israelite tradition. We may also ask whether this thinking-together was a late process only, or whether people had not already been aware much earlier of the connections between the terms and formulations in which God's relations to Israel were expressed—indeed whether the exact

---

[7] See, e.g., K. Baltzer, *The Covenant Formulary* (ET 1971).

[8] Brief but clear pointers to the connection between these three themes can be found in S. Herrmann, 'Die konstruktive Restauration: Das Deuteronomium als Mitte biblischer Theologie' in *Gesammelte Studien* (1986), 170f.

[9] It is missing from the index of biblical references in L. Perlitt's book *Bundestheologie im Alten Testament* (1969), for example, but also from A. H. J. Gunneweg's *Biblische Theologie des Alten Testaments* (1993), to name only two instances.

opposite is not the case: whether the different formulations were not merely different ways of expressing a great theme whose inner cohesion was never in doubt.

At the very least, a theological interpretation of the Old Testament must not allow itself to be hindered by either historical or form criticism from reading and interpreting the texts in the contexts in which they are now given to us. In this process the observations which have been made in the light of historical and form-critical questions will undoubtedly have to be taken into account. But they can only have a subordinate function, and must ultimately contribute to a better understanding of the text in its final form.

II

A NEW LOOK AT 'THE COVENANT FORMULA'

1. *Introduction*

a) The History of Research

That Yhwh is Israel's God, and Israel Yhwh's people is one of the central statements in the Old Testament. It is expressed in a variety of linguistic forms. Among these one characteristic phrase, almost formula-like in character, stands out clearly: 'I will be God for you and you shall be a people for me.'[1] Rudolf Smend was the first to subject this formula to a closer investigation, and through his study the term 'covenant formula' has come to be a generally used designation.[2] Yet this formula is by no means linked directly in every instance with the Hebrew word $b^e r\hat{\imath}t$, which is generally translated as 'covenant'.[3] In spite of this, there is much to be said for retaining the expression 'covenant formula'. For one thing, it is not, in my view, desirable to abandon without a compelling reason terms which have found their way into research, since to do so gives rise to unnecessary confusion.[4] For another, I hope to show that the link between the formula and the term $b^e r\hat{\imath}t$, and what it means, is in fact closer than is often assumed.[5]

In highlighting the formula, Smend followed the example of Julius Wellhausen. He went an important stage further than Wellhausen in his investigation, however. He writes: 'Wellhausen would have thought it beneath his dignity to investigate in detail formula-like material of this kind, which can be said from the outset to express merely what can be deduced without difficulty from the Old Testament as a whole'.[6] It should be added that this kind of investigation of formula-like material

---

[1] The somewhat clumsy translation follows the structure of the Hebrew sentences.

[2] R. Smend, 'Die Bundesformel', *ThSt(B)* 68 (1963).

[3] N. Lohfink has put together the instances in clearly surveyable form in 'Dt 26,17–19 und die "Bundesformel"', *Studien zum Deut.* 1 (1990), 215.

[4] E. Kutsch suggested the phrase 'affiliation formula' (*Zugehörigkeitsformel*), because he would like to avoid the term 'covenant'; see his *Verheißung und Gesetz* (1973). But in my view this phrase does not cover the mutuality which is expressed in the two-term version of the formula. There it is not so much a formula of 'belonging to' as of 'belonging together'.

[5] For example, H. H. Schmid, 'Ich will euer Gott sein und ihr sollt mein Volk sein', in *Kirche. Festschrift G. Bornkamm* (1980), 16, calls this bond 'extremely loose'.

[6] Smend, 'Die Bundesformel', 12.

was in any case outside the bounds of Wellhausen's methodology and interest, and that with his study Smend took the next step in the history of research. His investigation had two methodological presuppositions: the insight contributed by form criticism into the significance of set phrases or 'formulas'; and the assumption that formulas, like other set texts, have a particular *Sitz im Leben*. His investigation therefore concentrated first on the only text which mentions a specific occasion for the solemn pronouncement of the covenant formula, the scene in Deut. 26.16–19; and his second concern was above all the age of the formula. Here the supposition that it was this very formula that was pronounced on Josiah's conclusion of the covenant in II Kings 23.1–3 plays an important part.[7]

As a result of this methodological approach, the other texts which come into question are considered solely from this point of departure. This has a number of consequences. The most important is that Smend chooses as his starting point the bilateral formula: 'I will be your God, and you shall be my people' (with its variations). From this point, the other formulas then appear under the form-critical aspect of 'a dissolution of the reciprocal character of the declarations'. This finds especially radical expression when he says that in the Deuteronomic-Deuteronomistic literature 'often only half the formula is used—the part in which Yahweh ordains that Israel will be his people'.[8] The counterpart to Deuteronomy is the Priestly Writing. It favours the other half of the covenant formula, 'so that I would be your God', dropping the other theologoumena which are contained in the full formula 'because they are no longer required'.[9]

This concept whereby the bilateral formula is judged the real main form, and the other two formulas are viewed as parts or 'halves' of this formula, has met with widespread approval. But if all the texts in question are closely investigated, it emerges that the term 'half' (which after all suggests a deficit or even a loss) does not do justice to the facts. In addition, the consideration of these phrases as set 'formulas' resulted, for the most part, in neglect of the context in each particular case. In what follows, therefore, I shall look at the texts in question without the premises of 'the whole formula' and its two 'halves', and shall especially look more carefully at the respective contexts.[10]

---

[7] Smend, 'Die Bundesformel', 33, starts from this assumption 'in full appreciation of its uncertainty'. The question was taken up critically and extensively by Lohfink in 'Dt 26,17–19 und die "Bundesformel"'.

[8] Smend, 'Die Bundesformel', 34.

[9] Smend, 'Die Bundesformel', 35.

[10] M. Greenberg, *Ezekiel 1–20* (1983), 254, gives a brief but highly instructive survey of the use of the covenant formula. A somewhat eccentric 'family tree' of the formula may be found in C. Levin, *Die Verheißung des Neuen Bundes* (1985), 106.

b) The Linguistic Form and the Instances

Let me begin with some comments about the linguistic form. Scholars are largely unanimous in defining the 'formula-like' instances,[11] and these display some characteristic linguistic elements. In a number of cases the verb היה, 'be', is followed by a double ל: לאלהים לך להיות, 'in order to be God for you'. This formulation can be found seven times (with a shift between לך, 'for you' singular, לכם, 'for you' plural, and להם, 'for them'),[12] while the corresponding formulation להיות לו לעם, 'to be a people for him', occurs six times (also with variants),[13] in different textual realms in each case. The verb היה, 'be', is used in the great majority of the other examples too; and in all the instances which can be termed formula-like the word אלהים, 'God', or עם, 'people', is preceded by the preposition ל, 'to' or 'for'. This shows that the formula never merely describes an existing condition, but always a process through which Yhwh becomes, or has become, Israel's God, and Israel becomes, or has become, Yhwh's people, whether it be in the past, present or future.[14]

We encounter the formula in three versions (with variants): (1) 'I will be God for you'; (2) 'You shall be a people for me'; (3) where the two statements are combined in *a single* formula, though here the sequence of the two elements changes. In order to avoid the conceptuality of 'full formula' and 'halves', I shall from now on call these three versions Formula A (= 1), B (= 2) and C (= 3).

There are striking differences in the incidence of the three formulas. Formula A (Yhwh's being God) occurs almost exclusively in the first four books of the Pentateuch.[15] In these books we do not encounter Formula B at all, but we do find the bilateral Formula C (twice).[16] In Deuteronomy the matter is reversed: Formula B (Israel's being a people) occurs several times;[17] Formula A, on the other hand, never; and Formula C again twice.[18] We may assume with certainty that here deliberate and theologically reflected differences are being expressed, especially since in both sectors we are looking at decidedly 'theological' texts: the Priestly stratum of the Pentateuch and the Deuteronomic texts.[19] In the prophetic books (above all Jeremiah and Ezekiel) it is

[11] See the survey in Lohfink, 'Dt 26,17–19 und die "Bundesformel"', 211.

[12] Gen. 17.7; Lev. 11.45, 22.33, 25.38, 26.45; Num. 15.41; Deut. 26.17.

[13] Deut. 4.20, 7.6, 14.2, 26.18; II Kings 11.17; Jer. 13.11.

[14] This also applies to the other verbs which are occasionally used for the formula (or the part of it) which is related to the people: לקח, Ex. 6.7; קום (Hiphil) Deut. 28.9, 29.12 <13>; עשה, I Sam. 12.22; כון (Polel), II Sam. 7.24.

[15] Gen. 17.7b, 8b; Ex. 29.45; Lev. 11.45, 22.33, 25.38, 26.45; Num. 15.41 (and also Ezek. 34.24).

[16] Ex. 6.7; Lev. 26.12.

[17] Deut. 4.20, 7.6, 14.2, 27.9, 28.9.

[18] Deut. 26.17, 19, 29.12 <13>.

[19] Cf. also Smend, 'Die Bundesformel', 34f.

almost exclusively the bilateral Formula C that is used (with the
exception of Formula A in Ezek. 34.24 and Formula B in Jer. 13.11).
Outside the textual sectors mentioned, we encounter the covenant
formula in scattered cases in the books of Samuel and Kings, and here
the relationship to certain texts of the Pentateuch is of particular
interest.[20]

2. *The Covenant Formula in the Priestly Pentateuch*

A Preliminary Comment

In the first four books of the Pentateuch we encounter the covenant
formula only in versions A and C, and exclusively in texts which in their
language and theology quite evidently belong to the 'Priestly' stratum.
The boundaries of this stratum are largely undisputed even in the most
recent discussion about the growth of the Pentateuch, because its
characteristics are extremely clear. What is disputed is the question
whether this is an independent 'source', which initially existed independently of the other Pentateuchal texts before it was united with them,
or whether we should rather think of a 'composition stratum', which
certainly has its own unmistakable features, but which at the same time
only acquired its form when it was worked into a whole with the other
texts (all of them older). I myself am assuming this latter position, as it
has been developed by Erhard Blum in particular.[21]

a) Genesis 17

In Genesis 17, God's *berît* with Abraham and his descendants is the
dominant theme. Twice the divine speech begins with the emphatic
form of 'I', אֲנִי,[22] and in both cases the covenant is the essential subject
of what is said. Its substance is first the promise of numerous descendants (vv. 2b, 4, 6). Then the speech about the covenant begins again,

---

[20] A number of different texts might be mentioned which are close to the covenant
formula in one way or another. Formally, Zech. 2.15 <11> is close to Formula B, but it is
talking about God's relationship not to Israel but—'in a final modification of the covenant
formula' (Smend, 'Die Bundesformel', 39)—to 'the nations'. Levin, *Die Verheißung des
Neuen Bundes*, 106, instances Ezek. 34.30, where the recognition formula is combined
with a statement about 'my people'. Lohfink, 'Dt 26,17–19 und die "Bundesformel"',
211, mentions Hos. 1.9 and 2.25 <23> as 'formulations which echo the formula' (Smend,
'Die Bundesformel', 16, also mentions these passages). In addition he instances Ps. 33.12,
95.7, 100.3. All these texts would have to be drawn upon in a more extensive
investigation.

[21] On these questions see R. Rendtorff, *The Problem of the Process of Transmission in
the Pentateuch* (ET 1990), esp. 136ff., and E. Blum, *Studien zur Komposition des
Pentateuch* (1990), esp. 221ff.

[22] Here I am following S. E. McEvenue's convincing analysis of the chapter in *The
Narrative Style of the Priestly Writer* (1971), esp. 160ff.

and even more solemnly: God establishes (הקים) his covenant (בריתי) as an 'eternal covenant' (ברית עולם) between himself and Abraham's descendants. The content of this covenant is '*to be God for you* and for your descendants after you' (v. 7). Here, therefore, there is a very close link between Formula A and the *berît* itself: Yhwh's being God for Israel is the substance of the covenant. Then comes an additional promise, the gift of the land, a promise which will be fulfilled only for Abraham's descendants (v. 8a). Finally the text repeats once more: '*and I will be God for them*' (v. 8b). Formula A is therefore used twice here, and frames the promise of the land. Here it is especially significant that in this case the covenant formula stands right at the beginning of God's history with Israel, as an explication of what God's *berît* means for Abraham and his descendants.

b) Exodus 6

The next passage in which we meet the covenant formula, Ex. 6.2–8, calls for a detailed examination. God's address to Moses begins with the 'self-introductory formula' אני יהוה, 'I am Yhwh'.[23] Here this is explicitly set over against the introductory formula in Gen. 17.1, 'I am El-Shaddai': the name Yhwh was still unknown to the patriarchs, but it is now ceremoniously revealed. This section of the text displays a highly planned structure: the formula 'I am Yhwh' occurs three times, as first (v. 2) and as last (v. 8) utterance in the divine speech, as well as the first saying in the address which Moses is told to pass on to the Israelites (v. 6). This 'I am Yhwh' is thus the framing theme, so to speak, of this central encounter of God with Moses, and through Moses with Israel.

The introductory revelation of the Name is followed by two parallel statements, which both begin וגם (literally 'and also', vv. 4 and 5). V. 4 again casts back to Genesis 17: God has established (הקים as in Gen. 17.7) his *berît* with them (i.e. Abraham, Isaac and Jacob, v. 3); here the promise of the land is named as substance of the *berît*, as it is in Gen. 17.8. The second sentence introduced with וגם (v. 5) then adds something new: God has heard the groans of the Israelites in Egyptian captivity, and—with this the statement looks back again to v. 4—has remembered his covenant. The narrator had already reported this in Ex. 2.24. Now God himself says it to Moses. What links these two sentences

---

[23] W. Zimmerli introduced the term 'self-introductory formula' in 'Ich bin Jahwe', in *Geschichte und Altes Testament: Festschrift A. Alt* (1953), 179–209. In the same essay (186ff. = *Gottes Offenbarung* (1963), 18ff.) he also gives a detailed analysis of Ezek. 6.2–8. See also J.-L. Ska, 'La place d'Ex 6,2–8 dans la narration de l'exode', *ZAW* 94 (1982), 530–548, and 'Quelques remarques sur Pᵍ', in A. de Pury (ed.), *Le Pentateuque en question* (1989), 95–125.

together, apart from the introductory וגם, is the reference to the *bᵉrît* which God has established and which he is now remembering.

With the transitional לכן, 'therefore', the charge to Moses begins: he is to talk to the Israelites (v. 6). This divine speech begins again with the emphatic 'I am Yhwh'. The reiteration of the self-introductory formula heralds a change of perspective: whereas up to now the past was the subject, now the announcement begins of what God means to do. The speech has initially two component parts. The first is the assurance that God will lead Israel out of Egypt, will deliver it from bondage, and with the demonstrations of his power will redeem it (v. 6). God thus draws the conclusions from his 'remembrance' of his covenant by announcing that he will save Israel. As second element in the divine speech, the covenant formula then follows, this time in the form of the two-part Formula C: '*I will take you for my people and will be God for you*' (v. 7a). What is unusual here is the verb לקח, 'take', which occurs in no other formulation of the covenant formula. But it is certainly not by chance that this word appears at this precise point, where God addresses Israel as people for the first time; for it is only in the immediately preceding narratives that Israel has in fact become a people (cf. Ex. 1.7, 9). Consequently it is also with good reason that in God's address to Abraham in Genesis 17 only Formula A about Yhwh's being God should be used; whereas now the two-part formula follows, with which Yhwh 'takes' the 'people' of Israel to be his people. We can also see why the second part of the formula, which talks about Israel's being a people, comes first; for it is this which embodies the new thing that is now announced.

The comparison with Genesis 17 brings out yet another difference. In Gen. 17.7 the covenant formula is mentioned first, as disclosure of the content of the *bᵉrît*; the practical promise of possession of the land then follows. In Ex. 6.6, on the other hand, the divine speech begins with the announcement of the specific act of deliverance; only after that does the covenant formula follow (v. 7a). There is therefore a kind of chiasmus between these two texts as far as the relation between covenant formula and the promise of God's act is concerned. In God's first address to Abraham, the decisive thing is the assurance of Yhwh's being God, an assurance which unfolds the substance of the covenant. This assurance is then endorsed through the promise of the land. Under the burden of Egyptian slavery, on the other hand, the promise of deliverance takes first place; it demonstrates, as it were, what is afterwards declared: Israel's acceptance as God's people, which is now solemnised. The comparison of these two texts therefore shows that the position of the covenant formula in its immediate context is a matter of very careful reflection.

The divine speech closes with a further formula-like element of Priestly language: 'the recognition formula', 'You shall know that I am

Yhwh your God'.[24] We meet this formula here for the first time in the Hebrew Bible, and in a form which is expanded several times. First of all we have the formula itself in its 'long' form, with the additional 'your God'. This is given its particular stress through the fact that this 'your God' follows immediately on the second part of the covenant formula: 'I will be God for you'. The Israelites will recognise that Yhwh is God for them from what he says about himself: 'who brings you out of the enslavement of the Egyptians' (v. 7b). This is a word-for-word repetition of the announcement of the deliverance from Egypt at the beginning of the address to Israel (v. 6), with only a change in the verb form (participle instead of consecutive perfect). In both cases the phrase 'I am Yhwh', which stands in an emphatic position at the beginning of the speech, is explicated by the announcement of the deliverance from Egypt.

In v. 8 the promise that Israel will be brought into the promised land then follows—a promise that goes beyond what is said in v. 6. This land is characterised as 'the land that I raised my hand [in an oath] to give to Abraham, Isaac and Jacob', an utterance which again links back to the beginning of the whole divine speech, which began with the naming of the patriarchs (v. 3).

Ex. 6.2–8 is therefore in several respects a key text. This is true not only of its position in the wider context of the Exodus narrative, but also and above all because of its central theological statements about God's relationship to Israel. The solemnity with which the name of Yhwh is introduced is at the same time reflected in the triple use of the self-introductory formula 'I am Yhwh'. The word $b^e r\hat{\imath}t$, 'covenant', is picked up out of the history of the patriarchs, and through God's 'remembrance' is carried further and made historically efficacious. Thus it is here for the first time that we meet the bilateral covenant formula, which could not appear earlier because it is only now that Israel has become a people. Finally, it is at this point too that we first encounter the recognition formula, which is given its particular stress here through its direct link with the covenant formula. Who Yhwh is, what he is for Israel, and what he will do for Israel: this is expressed here with the most extreme linguistic and theological concentration. The density of the formula-like elements, which are a characteristic of the Priestly language, shows that this text, which is theologically so important, has been formulated throughout with especially scrupulous care.

c) Leviticus 26

We meet the bilateral Formula C once more in Leviticus 26, the great

---

[24] For details see W. Zimmerli, *Erkenntnis Gottes nach dem Buche Ezekiel* (1954).

concluding chapter of the law-giving on Sinai.[25] If we make the passage
begin with 25.55, as do some scholars, then it begins with three
sentences, each of which ends with the self-introductory formula 'I am
Yhwh' (25.55; 26.1, 2). The Masoretic division of the text, however,
takes back these three verses to what has gone before, and makes the
new *parashah* then begin with 26.3. In either case these three sentences
form the transition to the great closing discourse, so that chapter 26 must
be read within the progression of thought which these sentences
introduce.[26] Its themes are: the deliverance of the Israelites from
Egyptian slavery (25.55), the prohibition of the manufacture and
worship of idols (26.1), and the obligation to keep the sabbath (26.2).
The last two inculcate two decisive commandments in the Decalogue,[27]
so that these become the key signature of the great final discourse.

This speech in chapter 26 presupposes the presence of the Israelites in
the land, which is voiced in 25.2: 'When you come into the land which I
give you'. The speech is divided into two main parts of varying length
which are introduced by אִם, 'if' (26.3), or וְאִם־לֹא, 'but if not' (v. 14),
respectively. If the Israelites keep the divine commandments and
statutes, God will give them blessing and peace in the land. These
promises culminate in the renewed confirmation of the *bᵉrît* (v. 9), and
here the verb הקים, 'establish', quite clearly means that the covenant
will be kept on God's side.[28] This adherence to the covenant means that
God commits himself to Israel and keeps the promise given to Abraham
that he will make Israel fruitful and multiply it (cf. Gen. 17.6); and it
also means the fertility of the land. But now a further decisive element is
added: God will take up his dwelling in the midst of Israel and 'will
walk in its midst' (התהלך, vv. 11f.). This goes back to Ex. 29.45f.,
which had already announced that God would dwell among the people
of Israel (see below).

At this point the two-part covenant formula now appears (Formula
C): '*I will be God for you, and you shall be a people for me*'. It is the

---

[25] I see Leviticus 26 as the end of the law-giving on Sinai as a whole and not, as is
widely thought, the end of the 'Holiness Code' (This was already my perception in *The
Old Testament: An Introduction*, 146). Apart from the fact that Leviticus 26, with its
extensive scope, would be a completely disproportionate ending for what is rather a mixed
collection of laws (and quite apart from my own doubt about the existence of a 'Holiness
Code' as an independent entity), essential statements in this chapter can be understood
only in the context of the Sinai narrative as a whole.

[26] There are also good reasons for viewing chapters 25 and 26 as a single rhetorical unit
which opens with the introductory formula 'Yhwh spoke to Moses on Mount Sinai' (25.1).
Cf. the discussion in J. E. Hartley, *Leviticus* (1992).

[27] It emerges here that—in spite of the antecedent history which was convincingly
worked out by Zimmerli in 'Das zweite Gebot', in *Festschrift A. Bertholet* (1950)—the
first and second commandment are regarded as a single commandment: the manufacture
and worship of idols offends against the command for the sole worship of Yhwh.

[28] Cf. J. Gamberoni, 'קום *qûm*', ThWAT 6 (1989), 1263.

second time that we have encountered this formula in the Pentateuch. Here it is quite obvious that there is a direct reciprocal relationship between this instance of the formula and its first appearance in Exodus 6.[29] In both cases the phrase 'I will establish [or keep] $b^e r\hat{\imath} t$' comes first. In both cases another formula-like self-utterance on Yhwh's part follows—in Ex. 6.7b in the form of the expanded recognition formula, in Lev. 26.12 in the form of the also-expanded self-introductory formula 'I am Yhwh, your God'. In both cases the expansion additionally takes in the relationship to the deliverance from Egypt, formulated in the same way (with הוֹצִיא, 'bring out').

There remains one difference between the two versions of the covenant formula. In Ex. 6.7 the words 'I am taking you to be a people for me' come first; in Lev. 26.12, on the other hand, the first words are: 'I will be God for you'. Lohfink writes here: 'This reversal is probably determined by the particular context'.[30] Where Exodus 6 is concerned, we have already tried to give a reason for the anteposition of the saying about 'taking you to be a people': it was only in Egypt that Israel became a people for the first time, and in addition this is the new statement over against Genesis 17. In Leviticus 26, the point is now that God is entering the land together with Israel, and is taking up his dwelling in its midst, thus endorsing and sealing his being God for Israel. Yhwh's being God for Israel is in the antecedent, emphatic position here because it is the essential presupposition for Israel's way to a life in the land under the blessing and peace promised by God.

d) Further Instances of Formula A

Between the two cornerstones of the two-part covenant formula C in Exodus 6 and Leviticus 26, we now encounter formula A in some further texts. First of all, God's taking up his dwelling in the midst of Israel, which plays so important a part in Lev. 26.11f., has already been made a specific theme in Ex. 29.43–46. There the instructions for the sanctuary that is to be set up are brought to a (provisional)[31] close with the assurance that in the future God will 'meet' Israel in his sanctuary, and will 'dwell' with it. This is given extra force by formula A: 'I will dwell in the midst of the Israelites, *and I will be God for them*' (v. 45). In the direct context of the directions for building the sanctuary, the

---

[29] Cf. Lohfink, 'Die Abänderung der Theologie des priesterlichen Geschichtswerks: Zu Lev. 26,9.11–13', in *Studien zum Pentateuch* (1988), 161.

[30] Lohfink, 'Die Abänderung der Theologie des priesterlichen Geschichtswerks', 161.

[31] Chapters 30f. of Exodus apparently belong to a 'later development'; cf. Blum, *Komposition des Pentateuch*, 307f., with notes.

essential point here is God's presence among his people, as a confirmation of his being God for Israel; this is expressed with formula A. As already in the case of formula C in Exodus 6, formula A is directly followed here by the recognition pronouncement: 'You shall know that I am Yhwh, your God' (v. 46). Here again this statement is expanded by the reference to the deliverance from Egypt, which is given an additional emphasis through the final clause: 'who brought them out of the land of Egypt *in order that I might dwell in their midst*'. Here God's dwelling among the people of Israel is actually termed the real goal of the deliverance from Egypt. The whole passage ends with the self-introductory formula: 'I am Yhwh, your God'. The reiteration of the statement about God's dwelling in the midst of Israel in Lev. 26.11 clearly shows the deliberate and well-considered interweaving of these formulas, and their structuring function for the composition of the whole textual complex which they frame.[32, 33].

In Lev. 11.44f. the first of the purity regulations ends with the demand: 'Be holy, for I am holy'. This phrase, which occurs twice (vv. 44a, 45b), frames formula A, which is again related to the deliverance from Egypt: 'For I am Yhwh, who has brought you out of the land of Egypt, *in order to be God for you*' (v. 45a). Here, therefore, it is Yhwh's holiness which is newly added to his being God, and gives rise to the demand that the Israelites themselves be holy. At this point Yhwh's being God for Israel thus appears as the actual purpose of the deliverance from Egypt: '*in order to be God for you*'. The whole passage is structured by the self-introductory formula which introduces it, here in the version 'For I am Yhwh, your God' (v. 44a), and is then repeated before the covenant formula in the shorter form 'For I am Yhwh'.

In a very similar way the final admonition after the enactments on sacrifice in Leviticus 22 links talk about the holiness of God in the midst of the Israelites and the deliverance from Egypt using formula A: 'I show myself as holy in the midst of the Israelites: I am Yhwh, who sanctifies you, who brought you out of the land of Egypt *in order to be God for you*; I am Yhwh' (v. 32f.). In Lev. 25.38, formula A is used with a double definition of purpose, as it were (with two infinitives with ל, 'to'): 'I am Yhwh, your God, who brought you out of the land of Egypt in order to give you the land of Canaan, *in order to be God for you*'. Here the gift of the land of Canaan and Yhwh's being God for Israel are closely related as the goal and purpose of Yhwh's acts on Israel's behalf.[34]

[32] Cf. B. Janowski, '"Ich will in eurer Mitte wohnen"', in *Gottesgegenwart in Israel* (1993), 138.

[33] Cf. Blum, *Komposition des Pentateuch*, 328.

[34] In Lev. 25.38, however, the formula has no recognisable concluding function. In Num. 15.40f., Formula A is again used with a concluding function in connection with the deliverance from Egypt and Yhwh's being God for Israel.

e) Leviticus 26.42–45

Finally, the appearance of formula A in Lev. 26.45 is important. We have already talked about the function of the bilateral formula C in v. 12, where it serves as conclusion to the law-giving on Sinai. In the great chapter 26 of Leviticus, however, there is now still another emphasis: after all the disaster that had previously been announced has fallen on Israel, and now that God has finally turned back to her, the covenant is again moved into the centre (vv. 42ff.). God does not break it, but remembers the covenant he made with the earlier generations whom he brought out of Egypt '*in order to be God for them*'. This passage shows very clearly that this is not just a 'half' formula, but that for Israel's destiny everything depends on the fact that Yhwh is and remains Israel's God.[35]

f) Summary

In the 'Priestly' texts from Genesis 17 to Leviticus 26, therefore, the covenant formula in its two versions A and C has been very deliberately introduced for well-considered theological reasons; it fulfils important functions in the theological composition of this whole complex.[36] In Genesis 17, formula A appears for the first time: Yhwh declares to Abraham that he will be his God and God for his descendants. This promise is the substance of 'the eternal covenant', the ברית עולם, which God 'establishes' between himself and Abraham, as well as Abraham's descendants. Exodus 6 corresponds to this first text. In this Exodus passage, the two-part formula C stands at the centre of a divine speech which gathers up a whole network of established theological utterances: the self-introductory formula, the covenant formula, the recognition formula—the whole being presented as the unfolding and continuing endorsement of the promise of the covenant given to Abraham. The second occurrence of the two-part formula C in Leviticus 26 again

---

[35] We may leave on one side here the question whether these are the words of a final, late editor, as Lohfink, following Elliger, thinks (see 'Die Abänderung der Theologie des priesterlichen Geschichtswerks', 168). For what the canonical text is undoubtedly saying is that at the end of the 'history of suffering ... the power of the covenant with the patriarchs [must] after all make itself felt'. E. Otto, 'Das Heiligkeitsgesetz Leviticus 17–26', in *Altes Testament: Forschung und Wirkung* (1994), reads the text quite differently, because he views Leviticus 26 as a component part of the 'Holiness Code' and sees here an antithesis to the theology of the Priestly Writing. At the same time, when he writes: 'YHWH renews his covenant from generation to generation, provided that Israel fulfils the law or repents', this is in clear antithesis to the pronouncement in v. 44 that God will not break his covenant, a statement that is not conditional.

[36] Here I am assuming that the 'Priestly' texts are not a 'source' which can be isolated, but that they form one of the two final composition strata for the Pentateuch as a whole: cf. Rendtorff, *The Old Testament: An Introduction*, 138 and passim; Blum, *Komposition des Pentateuch*, esp. 219ff.

corresponds to Exodus 6, so that these two texts span the great complex from the announcement of the deliverance from Egypt until the close of the law-giving on Sinai. Between these two points, further stresses are placed by way of formula A: Yhwh takes up his dwelling in the midst of the Israelites (Exodus 29) and sanctifies them (Leviticus 11.22).

It is certainly not fortuitous that at the most important points the covenant formula should be directly linked with the term *berît*: in Genesis 17, on its first occurrence; in Exodus 6 and Lev. 26.12, where it appears in its two-part form; and in Lev. 26.45, which confirms that God himself will never break the covenant. Here covenant formula and 'covenant' form an indissoluble cohesion.

3. *The Covenant Formula in Deuteronomy*

a) Formula B

The context in which the covenant formula appears in Deuteronomy is of a completely different kind. At first we encounter the formula only in version B. The passage in which it first occurs, Deut. 4.20, is emphatically instilling the importance of the worship of God without images, which is stressed as the specific differentiation between Israel and all other peoples (v. 19b): 'Yhwh has taken you (לקח[37]) and brought you forth (ויצא) out of the iron furnace, out of Egypt, *in order that you should be the people of his own inheritance*'. Israel is to be God's people: that is presented here as the real purpose of the deliverance from Egypt. It is precisely this which shows the different emphasis of the passage compared with the instances in the books of Genesis to Numbers, where the purpose of the deliverance from Egypt is several times said to be that Yhwh desired to be Israel's God (Lev. 11.45, 22.33, 25.38; Num. 15.41).

For Israel, to be God's people means in particular keeping his commandments, the first (and second) commandment above all. In this respect Deuteronomy 4 with its context is to some extent close to Leviticus 26, which also begins with the rejection of idols and idol worship. Here in Deuteronomy 4 the term 'people' is even more closely defined as 'people of his inheritance' (נחלה). The term thus becomes at the same time a term of demarcation: Israel as God's people is distinct from the other peoples.

In Deut. 7.6 we also meet formula B in a context where the subject is Israel's cultic differentiation and demarcation over against the other peoples. This is very emphatically impressed on the Israelites in the first verse of the chapter, the stress lying on the sweeping away of foreign altars and cultic symbols. Here Israel's special status is described with the technical term בחר, 'choose': 'Yhwh has chosen you *to be a people*

---

[37] It is interesting that the verb לקח, 'take', should also appear in Ex. 6.7.

for his own possession, out of all the peoples that are on the face of the earth'. Here, therefore, the covenant formula (in version B) has entered into an intimate connection with the specifically Deuteronomic idea of 'election'. This is even more closely defined through the pronouncement that Yhwh has chosen Israel to be 'a people for his own possession' (עם סגלה). Here the phrase evidently has the same function as the related designation עם נחלה in 4.20.[38, 39]

The whole statement in 7.6 is introduced by the declaration: 'For you are a holy people for Yhwh your God'. 'Holy people' (עם קדוש) is a quite specific Deuteronomic expression.[40] Here it is an integrating component of the sentence structure, so that this statement embodies a very densely woven interlacing of the descriptions of Israel as a 'holy people' and as a 'people for [Yhwh's] possession'—the idea of election and the covenant formula (version B). The term berît can be found in the wider context too. In the subsequent explanation of Israel's special position, the oath God swore to the patriarchs is given as the reason why God brought Israel out of Egypt (v. 8). In v. 9 a 'recognition declaration' then follows, in which the epithets applied to Yhwh include the attribute שמר הברית, 'keeper of the covenant'. In this way the word berît belongs to one and the same thematic context as the covenant formula. What is also interesting is that immediately beforehand we find the prohibition of a berît with 'the peoples' (v. 2).

In 14.2 we encounter a further statement which is identical with 7.6, except for minor variations. In the section 14.1–21 the subject is also the cultic and religious separation, which is initially given concrete form in connection with mourning customs (v. 1), and then particularly with reference to the distinction between clean and unclean animals. The special importance of the latter distinction is lent extra force through the repetition at the end, in v. 21, of the phrase about the 'holy people' from v. 2, which thus forms a kind of framework for the exposition about clean and unclean animals.

Now it is particularly interesting here that the regulations about the distinction between clean and unclean animals are in part repeated word for word in Leviticus 11, but that there they are linked not with formula B but with formula A. In Leviticus too the sentence is long and complex, beginning with the 'self-introductory formula' אני יהוה and defining Israel's holiness on the basis of the holiness of God: 'For I am

---

[38] It is hard to detect a difference between the two, or a reason for the change from the one to the other: cf. Lohfink, 'Dt 26,17–19 und die "Bundesformel"', n. 90.

[39] Here the proximity to Ex. 19.4–6 is important. There elements of the covenant formula and elements of election terminology are also present, but without the strict formula-like phraseology. Smend, 'Die Bundesformel', 13, calls it a 'softened form', thereby assuming that it is later than the set formula. But that is by no means certain. Cf. also G. von Rad, *Das Gottesvolk in Deuteronomium* (1929), 10, n. 5.

[40] Deut. 7.6, 14.2, 21, 26.19, 28.9. Outside Deuteronomy, only the expression עם הקדש in Isa. 62.12 comes close to it, and also the singular גוי קדוש in Ex. 19.6.

Yhwh, your God. Sanctify yourselves therefore, and be holy, for I am holy . . . For I am Yhwh, who brought you up out of the land of Egypt *in order to be God for you*. Be holy, for I am holy' (vv. 44a, 45). In Leviticus 11, that is to say, the stress lies on God's holiness—in Deuteronomy 14 on the holiness of Israel.[41] But Leviticus 11 has to do with Israel's holiness too, for this is supposed to reflect the holiness of God. Apparently each writer could express what he found important in his particular context by way of the formula he uses.

We find formula B in two other passages in Deuteronomy. In 27.9, Israel as a whole is reminded by Moses and the Levitical priests: 'This day *you have become a people for Yhwh your God*'. This is linked with the admonition to keep the commandments (v. 10). In 28.9, in the light of the impending possession of the land by the obedient people, the text reads: '*Yhwh will raise you up* (הקים) *to be a holy people for himself*', with the coda 'as he has sworn to you'. Here too reference to the keeping of the commandments follows, and also that 'the peoples' are to see 'that you are called by Yhwh's name' (v. 10). So the covenant formula is again used in conjunction with the description of Israel as a 'holy people'. In addition this passage talks about Yhwh's oath, as did 7.8.[42]

b) Formula (A or) C

The complex text Deut. 26.17–19 makes it evident that the author of Deuteronomy also knew formula A. Here Formulas A and B are separated, but they are directly related to each other: '*to be God for you*' (v. 17)—'*to be a people for his possession*' (v. 18, again in the expanded form with the term עם סגלה, 'people for his possession'). The most striking feature here is that the two formulas are pronounced by different speakers: Israel and Yhwh.[43] The context describes the event of a ceremony with reciprocal obligations. For present purposes, we may set aside the question whether an actual rite for concluding a covenant lies behind this description.[44] What is important, however, is the observation that here the two formulas are not uttered by *a single* speaker—God, or someone whom he has charged to speak on his behalf (in the Pentateuch, Moses)—as is invariably the case when the two formulas appear together as *a single* formula, C; but that here they are pronounced by two different speakers, Israel and Yhwh. This, however,

---

[41] In Deuteronomy God is never called 'holy'; cf. J. G. Gammie, *Holiness in Israel* (1989), 108.

[42] See p. 63 below.

[43] The precise meaning of the Hiphil of the verb אמר, which occurs only here in the Hebrew Bible, remains a matter of dispute. Cf. the detailed discussion in Lohfink, 'Dt 26,17–19 und die "Bundesformel"', 229–235.

[44] Cf. here Smend, 'Die Bundesformel', and Lohfink, 'Dt 26,17–19 und die "Bundesformel"'.

means that here Israel itself declares that it wishes to be a people for God's possession. In the context of Deuteronomy as a whole, this would appear to be an explicit declaration on Israel's part that it desires to accept its special position as a people for Yhwh's possession and a holy people (v. 19)—a position that has been conferred on it several times previously—and that it will comply with this position by fulfilling the Torah.[45] The dipartite character of the formula—or, to be more precise, the two corresponding formulas—also make the bilateral nature of this procedure clear. Israel expresses this obligation in response to Yhwh's preceding declaration that he will be Israel's God. This reference to God's earlier promise is also explicitly mentioned: 'as he has promised you' (v. 18aβ; cf. v. 19bβ). But at the same time, for Israel itself to declare that it wishes to be God's people is the exception.[46]

We might perhaps ask whether it is justifiable to call formulas A and B a single formula, when in this text they are set over against one another. If we compare the other examples of the two-part formula C, we should rather have to answer this question with 'no'. Above all, there seems to be no very good reason for making this text the starting point and yardstick for all other instances of the bilateral formula.[47] Even in Deuteronomy itself, however, there is another example of formula C in the version otherwise generally used, in which Yhwh himself is the speaker, or the acting subject, for both parts of the formula. In Deut. 29.11f. <12f.> we read that Yhwh makes (כרת) a covenant with the fully assembled people of Israel, 'in order this day to raise you up (הקים) to be a people for him, *and he will be God for you*'. Here formula C is again very closely linked with the *bᵉrît*, and in this case the way the covenant is made is put down explicitly to God's oath to the patriarchs.

c) Summary

In Deuteronomy the covenant formula in version B predominates—the version stating that Israel is to be a people for Yhwh. This is God's gift and act of preference, over against the other peoples, a fact that is also expressed in the several times repeated expansion of the covenant formula in which the word סגלה, 'possession', or נחלה, 'heritage', is added to the word 'people'. But at the same time this preference for Israel also involves a limitation, which constitutes an important component in the commandments that grew up out of this preferential treatment. The requirement to keep the commandments is therefore also an essential element in the narrower definition of what it means to be a

---

[45] Cf. also F. Crüsemann, *The Torah* (ET 1996), 269ff.

[46] On II Kings 11.17, see below.

[47] Surely the fact that the reconstructed formula 'looks more original' than those frequently attested in actual fact (Smend, 'Die Bundesformel', 16) can scarcely count as a cogent argument.

people for God's possession. Towards the end of Deuteronomy, the other side of the covenant formula then appears as well, on the one hand in the unusual duality of the speakers (26.17–19), and then, at the end (29.11f. <12f.>), in the two-term declaration with the *one* acting subject Yhwh, the form which is usual in the rest of the Old Testament.

If we look back from this point, we can see that the covenant formula spans the whole history of God with Israel as it is presented in the Pentateuch, from the beginning of God's address to Abraham (Genesis 17), by way of Israel's emergence as a people in Egypt (Exodus 6), down to the border of the promised land (Deuteronomy 29). And it is precisely here, at the salient points of this history, that the bilateral formula C appears. It is very closely linked with the concept of the *b^{e}rît*, the covenant. In Exodus 6 it is God's 'remembrance' of his covenant with Abraham and the patriarchs which makes him intervene and bring the people out of Egypt. In Exodus it is at first only Moses who is told. But in Deuteronomy 29, at the end of the long journey, the new generation for whom the entry into the promised land is impending is then again admitted into this covenant relationship. In both cases, the bilateral covenant formula is at the centre of what God says (or Moses, aś the case may be), and in both cases the formula elucidates, as it were, what *b^{e}rît* means. Between these two cornerstones, we encounter the bilateral formula at still another key point: at the end of the law-giving on Sinai, in Leviticus 26. Here too it is something like an exposition of the way in which God's *b^{e}rît* with Israel shows and proves itself (v. 9): God will bring the people safely into the land, will dwell among them, and they will always remember that he brought them out of Egypt. Again the formula is at the centre (v. 12).

It emerges, then, that the covenant formula is an important element in the theological structuring and accentuation of the Pentateuch. Its description as 'covenant formula' proves to be completely justifiable, since at a whole series of central points it is used in direct association with the term 'covenant' (*b^{e}rît*)—indeed it not infrequently acts as something like its explication. At the same time, the presumption of their belonging together must not be overstressed, since the covenant formula and talk about the *b^{e}rît* each has its own profile, and to some extent the two certainly appear independently of one another.

Excursus: Exodus 19.4–6

When examples of the covenant formula are gathered together, the passage Ex. 19.4–6 is assigned a special position. Smend calls the text the (only) example of 'softened forms' of the covenant formula,[48] but gives it

---

[48] Smend, 'Die Bundesformel', 13.

no further consideration. Lohfink places it in the group 'Israel as Yah-weh's people', following it with a question mark in brackets (also as unique), and characterises it as 'an echo ... in relatively loose form'.[49] This is a way of saying that the text is close to instances of the covenant formula, but that the question whether or not it should be numbered among these can be answered in different ways. Here the descriptions 'softened' or 'loose' both assume that Ex. 19.4–6 is a later formulation than the 'normal' forms, and has already lost some of their characteristics.

Ex. 19.5b runs: והייתם לי סגלה, 'you shall be to me (for) a possession'. That is to say, the word סגלה, 'possession' (which we encounter several times in Deuteronomic phraseology), occurs here, but without the preceding word עם, 'people', and also without the preposition ל, 'for', which is otherwise generally used. The proximity to the Deuteronomic formulas is also evident in the additional phrase מכל־העמים, 'out of all peoples'. In this respect this text is close to the formulations in Deut. 7.6 and 14.2, but also to those in 26.19 and 4.20. Moreover, Ex. 19.6a has the phrase גוי קדוש, 'holy people', the sole occurrence of this expression in the Hebrew Bible; but this is very close to the formulation עם קדוש in Deut. 7.6, 14.2, 14.21, 26.19 and 28.9, which is also specific to Deuteronomy. The text displays other marked Deuteronomic formulations too, when it talks about 'listening to my voice' (Ex. 19.5a; cf. 'Listen to Yhwh's voice' in Deut. 13.19 <18>, 15.5, 27.10, 28.1 and passim) and also goes on to speak of 'keeping my covenant'; for in most of the Deuteronomic passages mentioned, the 'listening' is also followed immediately by 'keeping', even if this refers to the 'precepts' too. The phrase שמר ברית, 'keep the covenant', on the other hand, echoes Gen. 17.9 and 10, so that here as well there is a terminological cross-link with the Priestly Pentateuchal texts.

What is important about this text, above all, is that here at a highly central point—the beginning of Israel's sojourn at Sinai[50]—essential substantial and formal elements of the covenant formula are present. Whether these 'do not yet' or 'do not any longer' exhibit the 'strict' form of the covenant formula is relatively unimportant for their theological 'placing' and evaluation. The divine speech begins with the cast back to the deliverance from Egypt (v. 4), and in this respect is again close to many of the more strictly formulated covenant formulas. Perhaps the unusual introduction 'You have seen' can be brought into a certain proximity to the formula-like phrase 'You shall know' (Ex. 6.7). The terminology is undoubtedly different, but the remembrance of what has been seen is surely supposed to awaken the people's awareness that it is God who brought Israel out of Egypt, making his power visible

---

[49] Lohfink, 'Dt 26,17–19 und die "Bundesformel"', 212f.

[50] Cf. also R. Rendtorff, 'Der Text in seiner Endgestalt ... Exodus 19', in *Ernten, was man sät. Festschrift K. Koch* (1991).

through this act. The words 'I brought you to myself'—again an unusual phrase—in a certain sense anticipates the motif of God's presence in the place to which Israel has now come, a motif which then finds expression in Ex. 29.45f. (cf. Lev. 26.11f.), in close association with the covenant formula; again the terminology differs.

Finally, it only remains to stress that here too the word $b^e r\hat{\imath}t$ plays an important part. Now, however, unlike the instances of the covenant formula we have looked at so far, the other side of the $b^e r\hat{\imath}t$ is in the foreground: Israel's keeping or preserving the $b^e r\hat{\imath}t$. This was already the case in Gen. 17.9f., where Abraham is called upon to keep the $b^e r\hat{\imath}t$ by way of the circumcision. We shall have to consider this question further in another connection.[51]

Taken as a whole, therefore, the divine speech in Ex. 19.4–6 occupies a special position. It shows that the essential declarations of the covenant formula are not restricted to their strict formula-like modes of expression. It shows too that this is true not only of individual statements but also and especially of the group of declarations which we find gathered together in many instances of the formula: God's people; the difference from other peoples; the deliverance from Egypt; the covenant. Finally, it seems highly significant that this text, which is so close to the covenant formulas, once again appears in a passage which occupies a key position in the composition of the Pentateuch.[52]

4. *The Covenant Formula in the Books of Samuel and Kings*

In the great narrative complex of 'the former prophets' or the 'Deuteronomistic History' we encounter the covenant formula in only a few passages. Of course the omission or infrequent occurrence of particular terms and phrases in particular parts of the Hebrew Bible often does not permit us to draw particular conclusions. But for all that, we may say here that the covenant formula was not among the favourite forms of expression in Deuteronomistic theology.

The first passage in which the formula occurs, I Sam. 12.22, has received little attention in exegesis. Hans Joachim Stoebe calls vv. 21 and 22 'an interpolation within an interpolation', using the formulation of Martin Buber, who said this about v. 21, where he perceived the sound 'of an important though probably post-exilic voice'.[53]

---

[51] See pp. 83ff. below.

[52] One could also draw here on a text such as Josh. 24.17f., which contains essential elements of the same tradition but without the formula-like characteristics; cf. Smend, 'Die Bundesformel', 16, 18; Lohfink, 'Dt 26,17–19 und die "Bundesformel"', 220.

[53] H. J. Stoebe, *Das erste Buch Samuels* (1973), 239; M. Buber, 'Die Erzählung von Sauls Königswahl', *VT* 6 (1956), 159.

Martin Noth calls v. 22 one of the instances which shows that Deuteronomy, 'following the earlier traditions, ... talks about Israel as "the people of God"'.[54] He therefore evidently views the verse as 'Deuteronomistic'.[55]

The passage vv. 20ff. has a highly pregnant function in the context of Samuel's farewell discourse. Samuel recalls in detail the sins of earlier generations and reminds the people that in spite of this God repeatedly brought about great acts of deliverance through the Judges (vv. 9–11). In contrast to that, the desire for a king is an especially great sin (vv. 12, 18). The people now confess that they have indeed committed this sin, and they beg Samuel for his intercession (v. 19). To this Samuel replies with the renewed admonition to serve Yhwh alone and no other gods (vv. 20f.), and with the assurance that Yhwh 'for his great name's sake' will not cast off his people *'for it has pleased Yhwh to make (עשה)* you a people for himself' (v. 22). The unusual verb יאל (Hiphil), which I have rendered here with traditional terminology as 'it has pleased him', expresses a resolve that lies in the past and cannot be expected with certainty: to decide, declare oneself prepared, and so forth.[56] Here it has to be understood as the reason for the preceding declaration, and its confirmation: God will not cast away 'his people' (thus already v. 22a), because he previously made this resolve. In the text's whole sequence of ideas, this implies a stress on the steadfast nature of God's faithfulness to his people, a reliability which is grounded on his own resolve and on his 'great name'.

David's prayer in II Sam. 7.18ff. is very different in kind. It is offered in praise of God's mighty acts, God's greatness, and the greatness of his people which is his work (v. 23). This praise flows into the covenant formula in its two-part version C, the first half in somewhat varied form: *'You have installed your people Israel for yourself to be your people for all time*, and you, Yhwh, have become God for them' (v. 24). The unusual verbal form וַתְּכוֹנֵן, 'you have installed' (roughly in the sense of 'established'), is apparently due to the context of the prayer, where v. 13 says (in the divine speech): 'and I will give the throne of his kingdom endurance (וְכוֹנַנְתִּי) for all time'. This is probably also the reason for the phrase עַד־עוֹלָם, 'for all time, for ever', which is unusual in the covenant formula. This use of the covenant formula shows that it was part of the vocabulary with which this author was familiar, and which he was able to apply. But for him it is evidently the language of prayer, without any particular *Sitz im Leben*. The context echoes Deuteronomy 4, above all with the

[54] M. Noth, *Überlieferungsgeschichtliche Studien*, vol. I (1943), 101.

[55] R. Smend, *Die Entstehung des Alten Testaments*, 4th edn. (1990), 121, ascribes Samuel's whole speech to his 'DtrN', the 'nomistic Deuteronomist'.

[56] Cf. A. S. Kapelrud, TDOT, vol. V., 357–358.

rhetorical questions in v. 23 (cf. Deut. 4.7f., 32ff.); but it is interesting that in II Samuel 7 the author should use the two-part covenant formula, whereas in Deut. 4.20 we find only formula B.[57]

Finally, the text in II Kings 11.17 presents a particular problem. Here the covenant formula appears in version B as a direct résumé of the content of the $b^e r \hat{\imath} t$ which the priest Jehoiada makes (כרת) 'between Yhwh, and the king, and the people': that they should '*be a people for Yhwh*'. But whereas the declaration that Israel is Yhwh's people always otherwise proceeds from God's side, here, as already in Deut. 26.18, it is the people themselves who express this fact by entering into the covenant. It must be said, however, that the text is not very precisely formulated. There are three parties to the covenant formula: Yhwh, the king and the people (and in addition the priest, as 'mediator of the covenant'), but there is only one statement which can be understood as a declaration of commitment, the statement made by the people. Substantially speaking, however, it is clear that the essential content of this covenant ceremony is that Israel desires to be God's people (again).[58] The context shows that this means above all the obliteration of the foreign cultic places (v. 18). At all events, it should be noted that II Kings 11.17 is the only passage apart from Deut. 26.18 in which the statement 'to be a people for him' appears as a declaration of will on Israel's part. And yet the contexts of the two passages are entirely different. Deuteronomy 26 is talking about Israel's position as 'a people for God's possession' and a 'holy people', as distinct from the other peoples (v. 19); II Kings 11 is concerned with a largely political decision: the removal of a non-Davidic monarchical rule (associated as it was with the introduction of non-Yahwist cultic practices) and the restoration of the previous state of things.

The three examples of the covenant formula in the books of Samuel and Kings can hardly be welded into a single group. They show the highly sporadic occurrence of formulations which have been harnessed together as the 'covenant formula' because of the way this phraseology is used in other passages. Whereas in II Sam. 7.24 we find the full formula C, with some special linguistic features occasioned by the context, I Sam. 12.22 presents a varied version of formula B, while in II Kings 11.17 this formula has shrunk to the absolute minimum (להיות לעם ליהוה) and, moreover, appears as a declaration on the part of the people themselves.

---

[57] Lohfink, 'Dt 26,17–19 und die "Bundesformel"', 223, reckons with the possibility that the use of the bilateral formula 'could be from the beginning an intentional play on the correspondence of the adoption formula in II Sam. 7.14', where there is also an equivalent mutuality between Yhwh and David.

[58] According to Lohfink, 'Dt 26,17–19 und die "Bundesformel"', 223, the formula is intended to express that 'it was the oath "about being a people for Yahweh"'.

5. *The Covenant Formula in the Book of Jeremiah*

a) Jeremiah 7.23 and 11.4

In the book of Jeremiah we encounter the covenant formula only in the two-term version formula C, with a single exception (13.11: formula B). On its first occurrence in 7.23, the formula appears in a quite different context from that of the texts we have treated up to now: in connection with the prophetic criticism of the Israelites' sacrificial practice. The chapter opens with 'the temple speech' (7.1–15). This is dominated by criticism of a temple cult without the performance of what God requires as right conduct in the community of men and women; and it announces as consequence the destruction of the temple and the exile of the Judaeans. At the centre of the second section (vv. 16–20) is the polemic against the cult of 'the queen of heaven', which again ends with a pronouncement of judgement on the whole land.

Then, in the third section (vv. 21–28), burnt offerings and sacrifices are contrasted with the 'real' will of God. Jer. 6.20 had already said that burnt offerings and sacrifices 'are not acceptable' to God, this being a negative form, as it were, of a Priestly formula confirming that a sacrifice is pleasing or 'acceptable' to God.[59] In 7.21ff. Jeremiah[60] puts the matter still more trenchantly. In a rhetorical 'not–but' figure, he contrasts the sacrifices with the true will of God: when God led Israel's fathers out of Egypt, what he required of them was not sacrifice (v. 22); he asked that they should listen to his voice (v. 23). This phrase, frequent in Deuteronomy (13.18, 15.5, 27.10, 28.1 and passim), also occurs in Ex. 19.5, in the chapter that introduces the great narrative complex about Israel's sojourn at Sinai. There the phrase 'If you listen to my voice' and its continuation 'and keep my covenant' is followed by God's promise: 'then you shall be my possession out of all peoples'. Jer. 7.23 now says that when God brought Israel's fathers out of Egypt he said to them: 'Listen to my voice, *then I will be your God and you shall be my people*'.

The two texts in Exodus 19 and Jeremiah 7 are therefore related inasmuch as the covenant formula is followed by the demand that the people listen to God's voice. This sounds almost like a presupposition, or even a condition, which must first be fulfilled before Yhwh can and will be Israel's God. We shall have to discuss this question later.[61] But the difference between the two texts is, first, that in Jeremiah 7 the bilateral covenant formula is used, as is the case throughout the book of

---

[59] Cf. R. Rendtorff, *Studien zur Geschichte des Opfers im Alten Israel* (1967), 256f.

[60] I am using the name 'Jeremiah' here to mean the 'canonical' Jeremiah, as we meet him in the book that has been passed down under his name. This by no means excludes the existence in the book of varying literary elements. But this plays no essential role for our present question.

[61] See pp. 83f. below.

Jeremiah, whereas in Exodus 19 we find only the (incomplete) formula B, according to which Israel is to be (the people of) God's possession; and secondly, in the context of Jeremiah 7 the word $b^e rît$ is missing, whereas in Exodus 19 it plays a central part.

In Jeremiah 11 the word $b^e rît$ is at the centre. Jeremiah is charged to preach about the covenant: 'Hear the words of this covenant!' (v. 2) The section 11.3–5 parallels 7.22f. in many respects.[62] Both texts talk about the words which God spoke 'to your fathers . . . on the day when I brought them out of the land of Egypt'. In both cases the text goes on: 'Listen to my voice!'—and the two-part covenant formula then follows.

Considering how close to one another these two texts are, it is striking that in Jer. 7.23 the covenant formula should begin with Yhwh's being God (part A of the formula), while in 11.4, on the other hand, it begins with Israel's being a people (part B of the formula). A comparison of the two texts shows that this difference corresponds to a difference in their structure. In 11.4 the demand 'Listen to my voice!' is followed by the clause 'and do all that I command you', and the text goes on: 'So you shall be my people'. In 7.23, on the other hand, the demand 'Listen to my voice!' is followed directly by the declaration 'So I will be your God'. It is only after the second part of the covenant formula that a demand is then made for the people to act or conduct themselves in accordance with what God has commanded. In each case, therefore, part B of the formula stands in direct proximity to the requirement for conduct in accordance with God's will. This makes it clear that in the two-part covenant formula the sequence of the two elements is by no means arbitrary, even if the indications offered by the structure of the text are not always as clearly evident as they are here.

In Jer. 13.11 we encounter the phrase לִהְיוֹת לִי לְעָם, 'to be a people for me', in a context which does not suggest that it should be seen as closely connected with the covenant formulas. In a highly complex sign action with a loincloth, Jeremiah is told that God has made the whole house of Israel and the whole house of Judah 'cling to himself', 'so that they may be *a people for me*, and a name, and a praise, and an adornment—but they did not listen'. Here Israel's being a people for God belongs to a quite different context from the context of the covenant formulas. Moreover the use of the phrase in a series, in association with other expressions, gives it a different emphasis.

b) Salvation Oracles

In Jeremiah 24 we find the covenant formula in a wholly new context. These are the first years of the exile, and Jeremiah sees in a vision two

---

[62] Cf. the table in W. Thiel, *Die deuteronomistische Redaktion von Jeremia 1–25* (1973), 149.

baskets of figs, some very good and some very bad. In the divine interpretative saying, the good figs are identified with the Judaeans in exile. They are told that God will look graciously on them and grant them the favourable destiny of a return to their own country. This proclamation reaches its climax in the sentence: 'I will give them a heart to know me, that I am Yhwh: *and they shall be a people for me and I will be God for them*, for they shall return to me with their whole heart' (v. 7). This salvation oracle is matched by a succeeding oracle of doom pronounced on King Zedekiah and the others who have stayed in Jerusalem or fled into Egypt.

Here the covenant formula points to the future. With that part of Israel that is going to return from exile, God will make a new beginning, which will again be subject to the covenant formula, as the summary expression of God's relationship to his people. This is in a way reminiscent of Lev. 26.45, where the covenant formula (in version A) also comes at the end of the long history of disaster. There it is linked with the announcement that God will remember his covenant. Here, in Jeremiah 24, the change which will take place in Israel itself is in the foreground: God will give the people a heart to know him; and they will turn back to him with all their heart. So the new heart will bring about knowledge. This phraseology echoes two formulas which we often encounter in the Priestly texts of the Pentateuch: the recognition formula, here shortened to the infinitive לדעת, 'to know', and the self-introductory formula, expanded by the frequent כי, 'that I am Yhwh'.[63] But what is new here is that all this is announced for a salvific future still impending, in which Israel will then also turn back to God with its whole and new heart. Because the point of this passage is this new heart of Israel's, part B of the formula comes first.

In Jeremiah 30–32 we encounter the covenant formula four times in all; this is the greatest concentration in the Hebrew Bible. Apparently the formula has an extremely fundamental importance for the salvation oracles of these chapters, as a summary way of expressing the future restoration and renewal of Israel's relationship to God. In 30.22 the formula comes at the end of the section that begins in v. 18 with the divine oracle formula, the section which announces the restoration of the 'tents' and 'dwellings' of Jacob and their inhabitants, and finally the restoration of their 'ruler'. The closing formula in v. 21 constitutes a caesura, however, so that the covenant formula in v. 22 stands in a certain isolation. However this may be judged under a diachronic

---

[63] Cf. here W. Zimmerli, 'Erkenntnis Gottes nach dem Buch Ezechiel', AThANT 27 (1954), 34 and 65 (= *Gottes Offenbarung* (1963), 73 and 108). These formulations are close to the 'Priestly' tradition. Thiel's view about 'the origin of verse 7 of D' starts among other things from the assumption that here 'the covenant formula [is present] as D element' (*Die deuteronomistische Redaktion von Jeremia 1–25*, 256). But the two-part covenant formula is *not* in fact a 'D element' (see Section 3 above).

aspect,[64] here the formula has what might be called a programmatic character for the restoration of Israel which is described in the context.

This is even more true of 31.1, where we find the covenant formula in an unusual expansion. Introduced by the eschatological formula 'at that time', and continuing with 'saying of Yhwh's',[65] it goes on, '*I will be God for all families of Israel, and they shall be a people for me*'. The unusual phrase 'for all families of Israel' no doubt has an interpretative function, which is to relate the restoration of 'Jacob' announced in the previous section (30.18ff.) to the whole of Israel. With this expansion, the covenant formula now comes at the beginning, in an emphatic antecedent position, before the wide sweep of the chapter about Israel's homecoming and restoration begins with a new divine oracle formula (31.2). From this initial motto-like saying, threads can be traced right through the whole chapter, for example under the term 'people': 'the people who escaped the sword' has found grace (v. 2); in the call to prayer, God is invoked: 'Yhwh, save your people, the remnant of Israel' (v. 7); and it sounds almost like a variant of the covenant formula when we read, 'For I will be a father to Israel, and Ephraim is my first-born' (v. 9).

In the saying about 'the new covenant' (31.31–34), the covenant formula is again right at the centre. As was already the case in 24.7, the decisive point is that it will be Israel's heart in which the knowledge of God is located. In 31.31ff., the theological weight of these declarations is quite essentially intensified through the introduction of the covenant in association with the Torah. The covenant formula (v. 33b) occupies a central position between the declaration that the Torah, as content of the covenant, will be written into the hearts of the Israelites (v. 33a), and the other declaration that they will all know God without any external help (v. 34). The first part of the formula, '*I will be God for them*', follows the announcement that God will put his Torah in their hearts; the second part, '*and they shall be a people for me*', is followed by the declaration that they will all know God.

Finally, in the section 32.36–44 the covenant formula is once again at the centre. God will gather those who have been scattered, and bring them back to Jerusalem: here this is summed up in the declaration, '*They shall be a people for me and I will be God for them*' (v. 38). Again the heart plays a decisive role (vv. 39, 40b), and the 'eternal covenant' which God is going to make with the people (v. 40a) is described in

---

[64] W. Rudolph, *Jeremia* (1958), 175, says: 'v. 22 is rightly missing in G'. Why rightly? And how did the verse get into M? W. Thiel, *Die deuteronomistische Redaktion von Jeremia 26–45* (1981), 21, is more cautious and discusses reasons for this 'addition, which ... eludes a closer designation'.

[65] The linking of these formulas is characteristic of the book of Jeremiah: cf. R. Rendtorff, 'Zum Gebrauch der Formel *nᵉʾum jahwe* im Jeremiabuch', ZAW 66 (1954), 28 (= *Gesammelte Studien* (1975), 257), n. 7.

unequivocally plain terms as a covenant of grace, from which God will not depart.

Within the book of Jeremiah, then, we find a significant shift in the use and function of the covenant formula. In both texts in the first part of the book, the formula is closely linked with the deliverance from Egypt and the demand made by God at that time that the people should listen to his voice. In this way the formula acquires a particular function in the prophetic judgement sayings, because in the prophet's view Israel has not obeyed God's voice. Chapter 24 marks the turning point: God's judgement has descended upon Israel, and now a dividing line is drawn between those who have been taken into Babylonian captivity and those who have remained behind in the land. The first group is now the bearer of the promise, and the covenant formula becomes a central saying of assurance, promising God's saving acts for the 'remnant' of the people. With this remnant he is beginning a new chapter in history and making a 'new covenant', in which the fulfilment of his commandments will follow simply of its own accord from the new knowledge of God.

6. The Covenant Formula in the Book of Ezekiel (and Zechariah 8.8)

In the book of Ezekiel, we encounter the covenant formula solely in the context of promises of salvation for the era following judgement and, with a single exception (34.24), always in the two-term form. Already in the period before the fall of Jerusalem, those who have been exiled to Babylon are promised (11.14ff.) that God will not be with the people who have remained in the home country, who arrogantly pride themselves on their possession of the land, but that he will bring back the exiles and will give them a new heart and a new spirit, so that they will live according to his commandments: '*And they shall be a people for me and I will be God for them*' (v. 20). Here the echoes of Jeremiah are quite evident (cf. especially Jer. 24.7, 31.31ff.).

In Ezek. 14.1–11, a harsh saying directed against the idol-worshippers closes with a salvation oracle for 'the house of Israel', who because of the judgement on the idolaters will be persuaded to cease turning away from God and thus polluting themselves, so that '*they shall be a people for me and I will be God for them*' (v. 11).

What had already been announced before the fall of Jerusalem (and that means: before the judgement pronounced on Israel had come into effect) for the time afterwards is taken up again after the city's fall.[66] God now acts 'for the sake of my holy name' (36.22f.). He fetches the Israelites back from the land of exile, purifies them and gives them a

---

[66] Cf. R. Rendtorff, 'Ezekiel 20 and 36:16ff. in the Framework of the Composition of the Book', in *Canon and Theology* (ET 1993, 1994), 190–195.

new heart and a new spirit, so that they may fulfil his commandments
and live again in the land of the patriarchs: '*And you shall be a people
for me, and I will be God for you*' (v. 28).

In the sign action with the two sticks in 37.15ff., the announcement of
the reunification of Israel and Judah culminates in the promise that they
will be *one* people with *one* king in *one* kingdom, and that God will
purify them from all impurity and sin, '*and they shall be a people for me
and I will be God for them*' (v. 23). In the continuation of this passage,
the subject is first of all the new king, 'the servant David' (vv. 24f.), and
this is then followed by the announcement of a new covenant which
God will make with those who have been saved: a 'covenant of peace'
(ברית שלום), an 'eternal covenant' (ברית עולם). And God will then set up
his sanctuary (מקדש), his dwelling (משכן) among the Israelites: '*And I
will be God for them and they shall be a people for me*' (v. 27). This is
the only passage in the book of Ezekiel where in the two-term covenant
formula the element of Yhwh's being God (element A) is put first. This
is entirely warranted, because the point here is that God is going to
dwell among the Israelites as a sign that he is their God. At the same
time the two variants of the covenant formula in vv. 23 and 27 form a
kind of chiastic *inclusio*.

Otherwise this text is closely related to the two instances of the
covenant formula in Ex. 29.45 and Lev. 26.12. Both belong within the
context of the announcement that God will take up his dwelling in
the midst of Israel. Exodus 29 talks here about 'sanctifying' (vv. 43f.),
as does Ezek. 37.28. In both texts we also find the recognition formula,
though with one essential difference: in Ex. 29.46 it is Israel that is to
know; in Ezek. 37.28 it is 'the peoples': 'The peoples shall know that I
am Yhwh who sanctifies Israel because my sanctuary will be for all time
in their midst.'

It is only once that the covenant formula appears in the book of
Ezekiel in a single-element form—in 34.24, in the form of formula A
(Yhwh's being God). The text is clearly related to 37.21ff., where the
future 'David' also plays a role in the announcement of the future. There
the declaration 'My servant David shall be king over them' (v. 24)
follows directly on the two-term covenant formula; but in 34.24 the two
statements about Yhwh's being God and David's being king are welded
together into a new two-term phrase: '*I, Yhwh, will be God for them* and
my servant David (will be) prince among them'. At this point the
explicit stress on Yhwh's being God serves above all as a legitimation
of the future ruler.[67] Here this ruler is not described as king (as he is in
37.24); he is given the title נשיא, 'prince' (as also in 37.25), which is

---

[67] One wonders whether it is pure chance that the name of Yhwh should occur only
twice in the covenant formula, and both times in direct association with David: II Sam.
7.24 and Ezek. 34.24.

then used throughout in the cultic blueprint of the future in Ezekiel 40–48.[68]

Zechariah 8.8—the sole example of the covenant formula in the prophetic books outside Jeremiah and Ezekiel—is interesting. Here at the end of the series of sayings in 8.1–8 there is a tersely formulated promise that those who have been scattered will be brought back to Jerusalem (vv. 7–8), and this promise flows into the covenant formula: *'They shall be a people for me, and I will be God for them* in faithfulness and in righteousness'. The closing addition of the weighty paired terms באמת ובצדקה, 'in faithfulness and righteousness', stresses the fixed character of the covenant as a declaration summing up God's relationship to Israel as the fundamental presupposition for her salvific future.

---

[68] W. Zimmerli, *Ezekiel*, vol. ii (ET 1983), 219, points to the relationship between this text and Hos. 3.5 and Jer. 30.9, where we find a similar link between God and king in expectations for the future.

III

THE COVENANT FORMULA IN ITS EXEGETICAL CONTEXT

The diverse relationships in which the covenant formula appears in conjunction with other formula-like elements and with central theological terms show that the declarations of this formula can express God's relations to Israel and Israel's to God in an extensive and comprehensive way. It is especially worth noting in this connection that the covenant formula almost never stands alone, and that it is often linked not only with one but with several other formula-like elements or expressions which touch on the relationships between God and Israel.

Let us make this clear to ourselves once more on the basis of some characteristic examples. Two of the fundamental terms used to express God's relationship to Israel can be linked with the covenant formula in a positively classic way: 'I am establishing my *covenant* between me and you ... in order to be God for you' (Gen. 17.7), and 'Yhwh your God has *chosen* you to be a people for his own possession' (Deut. 7.6). The terms ברית and בחר, 'covenant' and 'choose', can be positively defined at central points through the covenant formula. An examination of Genesis 17 showed that there the covenant formula A is used twice, and embraces the promise of the land in a kind of *inclusio* (vv. 7f.). That is to say, the substance of the covenant is Yhwh's being God for Israel, this taking concrete form in the promise of the land. In Daniel 7 it is the concept of the 'holy people', the עם קדוש, which is spelled out more closely in the declaration about Israel's election by Yhwh, a pronouncement defined through the covenant formula B. This is followed by a passage arguing that God's elective act is founded on the performance of the divine oath to the patriarchs, and the consequent deliverance from Egypt. Although the terminology differs, the two texts nevertheless show that the promise of the land and the fulfilment of that promise through the deliverance from Egypt are key facts, in the light of which God's relation to Israel is continually viewed.

At the same time, these examples also make it clear that in every case the covenant formula has its significance and function in the context of the particular theological conception with which it is associated. It acts as a bridge between different theological ideas, while leaving each of them its own particular character.

1. *A Transitional Reflection: 'In Order To Be'*

One characteristic of the covenant formula is that in a great many instances it is introduced by the verb הָיָה, 'be', in the infinitive construct and with an antecedent לְ, 'in order to'. A closer examination shows that this phrase can be found only in texts belonging to the Pentateuch.[1] In the prophetic books, in contrast, the two-term covenant formula is always formed with the perfect consecutive and a succeeding imperfect: וְהָיִיתִי ... וְאַתֶּם תִּהְיוּ, 'I will be ... and you shall be', or vice versa, and with variants in the third person. I shall come back to this at the end of this chapter. It is noticeable in addition that in the Pentateuch the covenant formula in the bilateral version C is introduced not by this infinitive construction, but by other phrases which are determined in each particular case by the context. I shall come back to this point as well.

Looking back at the texts which we have hitherto considered in detail, it is now interesting to see what the phrase 'in order to be' refers to in each case. Let us look first at the texts with formula A, about Yhwh's being God.[2] Gen. 17.7 says that God is going to establish his *bᵉrît* as an 'everlasting *bᵉrît*', '*in order to be God for you* and for your descendants after you'. Here Yhwh's being God for Israel is as such the substance and purpose of the *bᵉrît*, the covenant. This pregnant formulation is undoubtedly quite deliberately and emphatically put at the beginning of the Abraham story, and thus at the beginning of Israel's history too; but in this form it remains unique.

Lev. 11.45 runs: 'For I am Yhwh, who has brought you out of the land of Egypt *in order to be God for you*'. Here Yhwh's being God for Israel is presented as being the purpose and goal of the deliverance from Egypt. The context is important in this case too, its theme being Yhwh's holiness and the requirement that the Israelites be themselves holy, a demand consequent on that. God has brought Israel out of Egypt in order to be God for Israel and in this way to bring it to 'holiness'. In Lev. 22.32f. the context is very similar: 'I am Yhwh, who sanctifies you, who brought you out of the land of Egypt *in order to be God for you*; I am Yhwh'. The purpose of the deliverance from Egypt is Israel's sanctification—its becoming holy through the being-God (*Gottsein*) of the holy Yhwh. Num. 15.40f. is similar: the pronouncement 'You shall be holy for your God' is followed by the declaration about the deliverance from Egypt, which goes on 'in order to be God for you'.

In Lev. 25.38 too, formula A follows the statement about the deliverance from Egypt. But here the definition of the deliverance's purpose is doubled, as it were (through a twice-repeated infinitive with לְ, 'in order to'): 'I am Yhwh your God, who brought you out of the land of Egypt in order to give you the land of Canaan, *in order to be God for you*'. The close link between the gift of the land and Yhwh's being God for Israel

---

[1] The sole exception is Jer. 13.11, a text which is not to be numbered among the 'covenant formulas'; see p. 32 above.

[2] See Chapter II, n. 15.

again emerges from the context. Leviticus 25 deals with questions about the possession of the land, these being gathered together under the heading: 'The land is mine; with me you are aliens and tenants' (v. 23). So possession of the land and dealings with it have as premise the fact that Yhwh, the giver of the land, is Israel's God.

In Lev. 26.45 the formula has a different emphasis. The context says that at the end of all judgements on Israel, God will remember his covenant with the patriarchs (v. 42) and will not break that covenant (v. 44). Remembrance of the covenant stands under the foretoken that God has brought Israel out of Egypt before the eyes of the peoples '*in order to be God for them*' (v. 45). Here too we find the link with the deliverance from Egypt; but in this context it is viewed primarily as a proof of Yhwh's power 'before the eyes of the peoples'.

That is to say, in the case of all the formulas in version A which are introduced by 'in order to be' there is a direct link with the deliverance from Egypt, with the sole exception of formula A's first occurrence, when it is addressed to Abraham (and hence before the sojourn in Egypt). But the deliverance from Egypt is not an end in itself, for Yhwh's being God always belongs in a particular context: the purpose is to give Israel the land (Lev. 25.38), to prove God's power before the eyes of the peoples (Lev. 26.45), or to let Israel share in God's holiness (Lev. 11.45, 22.32f.; Num. 15.40f.; for Deut. 26.17 see below).

In Deuteronomy, formula B, about Israel's being a people for Yhwh, serves essentially to separate Israel from other peoples. In addition, in the first instance, Deut. 4.20, the text is again talking about the deliverance from Egypt: God has commanded the stars of other peoples to worship him. 'But Yhwh has taken you and brought you out of the iron-smelter, out of Egypt, *in order that you should be the people of his own inheritance*'. According to this, the purpose of the deliverance from Egypt is that Israel, as distinct from other peoples, should be the people for God's own possession. A comparison with the instances of formula A, which always talk about the deliverance from Egypt, shows that formulas A and B view the purpose of this divine act from its two sides: as the foundation for Yhwh's being God for Israel, and as the foundation for Israel's being a people for Yhwh.

The two almost identically worded texts in Deut. 7.6 and 14.2 have a different emphasis. In these texts the covenant formula is linked with the concept of the election (בחר) out of all peoples, as well as with the idea of the 'holy people' and of 'possession', but without any reference to the deliverance from Egypt: 'For you are a holy people for Yhwh your God; Yhwh has chosen you *to be a people for his own possession*, out of all the peoples that are on the face of the earth'. This sentence is often viewed as the *locus classicus* of the election pronouncements in Deuteronomy, and the covenant formula (version B) is an integral part of it.

We are left with the two formulas A and B in their special ceremonial context in Deut. 26.17f.: '*to be God for you*' and '*to be a people for his own possession*'. Here both parts of the formula have to do with Israel's obligation to keep the divine commandments, which in the section vv. 16–19 are called, in the multiplicity of Deuteronomic terms, 'statutes, commandments and ordinances'. In this connection Israel's special position is stressed twice, with an explicit reference back to what was said earlier ('as he said'): Israel as 'a people for his own possession' (v. 18), and its exaltation above all peoples to be 'a holy people for Yhwh'.

Finally, formula C in Deut. 29.12 <13> must be mentioned here. It is a different formulation linguistically, but the introductory למען also expresses the element 'in order to'. In spite of the different formulations, a striking parallel to Gen. 17.7 emerges, inasmuch as the relationship between God and Israel which is expressed in the covenant formula is described directly as the substance of the *bᵉrît*.

Outside the Pentateuch, we encounter the covenant formula with the phrase להיות only in II Kings 11.17, with formula B, as a declaration about the covenant which King Jehoiada makes. Here the content of this covenant is given no more precise definition. But the context suggests that it is a matter of the restoration of the purity of the cult, i.e., pre-eminently observation of the first commandment.

Thus different aspects of the final or purposive 'in order to be' emerge in the covenant formula: the deliverance from Egypt points both towards Yhwh's being God and Israel's being a people; Israel's election is the foundation of its being a people for Yhwh; both aspects of the covenant formula have fundamentally to do with Israel's observance of the divine commandments; and finally, the covenant itself is the foundation for Yhwh's being God for Israel.

In the two-term version C, the covenant formula is not ushered in by 'in order to be' but is introduced in accordance with its context in each particular case. In the context of the announcement of the deliverance from Egypt, Ex. 6.7 begins: '*I am taking you to be my people*', the continuation being introduced by 'and I will be'; in Lev. 26.12 the covenant formula is a component in a series of perfect consecutives, and is accordingly introduced by והייתי, 'I will be';[3] in Deut. 29.12 <13> the *bᵉrît* which Yhwh is making with Israel 'today' is explicated through the covenant formula, which is introduced by a final or purposive למען, 'in order to'.

In the prophetic books, the two-term covenant formula is always formed with the perfect consecutive followed by an imperfect: ... והייתי ואתם תהיו 'I will be ... and you shall be', or vice versa, with variants in the third person. Here the formulations in the texts which go back to the

---

[3] In Ex. 29.45 this is so in the case of formula A as well.

deliverance from Egypt—those, that is, which look to the past (Jer. 7.23, 11.4)—are the same as the formulations in those texts which announce a new beginning in the relationship between God and Israel in the future, as do the remaining texts. We shall have to consider this point more closely.

2. Covenant Formula and 'Covenant'

Our survey of examples of the covenant formula has shown that in a whole series of texts there is a direct relationship to the catchword $b^e r\hat{\imath}t$. We must now follow this up in more detail.[4]

The link between the covenant formula and the $b^e r\hat{\imath}t$ dominates the Priestly Pentateuch. In Gen. 17.7 Yhwh's being God for Israel is stressed in formula A as being the real substance of the $b^e r\hat{\imath}t$: '*in order to be God for you*'. This is the first occurrence of the covenant formula in the Pentateuch, and has accordingly extreme weight. In addition, however, the term $b^e r\hat{\imath}t$ has a number of other aspects here, which we shall have to discuss in another connection.[5] The next occurrence of the covenant formula, in Ex. 6.7, belongs within a context which expressly points back to the $b^e r\hat{\imath}t$ made with Abraham (v. 4), which God now 'remembers' (v. 5b). The covenant formula then follows in a speech made by Moses to the Israelites; this is introduced by לכן, 'therefore', and is thus presented as being a consequence of remembrance of the covenant. Again, therefore, covenant formula and $b^e r\hat{\imath}t$ are closely interwoven. The third occurrence of the formula, in Lev. 26.12, is clearly related to Exodus 6; the formula appears in a passage which, like Ex. 6.4 and Gen. 17.7, begins with the phrase 'and I am establishing my covenant' (v. 9b). The renewed occurrence of the covenant formula in this chapter, this time in version A (Lev. 26.45), belongs in a sentence which begins with the phrase, reminiscent of Ex. 6.5, that God will remember his $b^e r\hat{\imath}t$. These four, theologically highly important instances of the covenant formula are therefore interconnected, and are all indissolubly linked with the term $b^e r\hat{\imath}t$.

In Deuteronomy, the connection between the covenant formula and $b^e r\hat{\imath}t$ is at first sight less marked. In Deut. 7.6 we find the covenant formula in a context where, in the framework of a recognition formula, God is described (v. 9) as 'keeper of the covenant'. According to the whole trend of the text, this 'covenant' is related through the recognition formula to the 'oath' mentioned in v. 8, which God swore to the patriarchs, an oath which he kept when he brought Israel out of Egypt.

---

[4] I have not given individual references to previous chapters, but suggest that the reader turn to the Contents and the Index of Biblical References.

[5] See below pp. 48 and 57 below.

The whole passage is part of a sustained argument about the reason why God chose Israel. This shows that here covenant formula and covenant belong to the same theological complex. Examination of the wider context shows that in chapter 4 too there is a connection between the covenant formula in v. 20 and the word $b^e r\hat{\imath}t$ in vv. 13, 23 and 31.[6] The link in 29.11f. <12f.> is much closer; there the covenant formula appears as the purpose of the $b^e r\hat{\imath}t$, as it were, being introduced by לְמַעַן, 'in order to'. In the other instances there is no detectable relationship between covenant formula and $b^e r\hat{\imath}t$.

In the book of Jeremiah, there are closer connections between covenant formula and $b^e r\hat{\imath}t$ in a large number of passages. In Jeremiah 11 the whole prophetic speech in vv. 2–10 falls under the catchword 'covenant'. The people addressed are told to listen to 'the words of this covenant'. They are the words which God spoke to the patriarchs when he brought them out of Egypt. The consequence of the listening is expressed in the two-part covenant formula (v. 4b). 'Listen to the words of this covenant' is also paralleled by 'Listen to my voice' (v. 4b). In 7.23 we find more or less closely corresponding statements, though without the use of the word $b^e r\hat{\imath}t$.

In Jer. 31.31–34 the relation between covenant formula and $b^e r\hat{\imath}t$ is quite central. The substance of the 'new covenant' will be that the Torah is put into the hearts of the Israelites. In this way a relationship between God and Israel will be established which is expressed in the covenant formula (v. 33). In 32.36–40 we find the same link, but described in converse form: the people who have been brought back from the dispersion will stand in the relationship to God which is expressed in the covenant formula (v. 38) and God will make an 'everlasting covenant' with them (v. 40). In this way these texts in the book of Jeremiah show that the covenant formula is very closely bound up with the theological context of the $b^e r\hat{\imath}t$. At the same time, we also find both the covenant formula and the word $b^e r\hat{\imath}t$ independent of one another in the book of Jeremiah.

In the book of Ezekiel there are two texts in which the covenant formula is linked with $b^e r\hat{\imath}t$. Both have to do with the future salvific condition in which a new David will rule over Israel. Ezek. 37.24ff. says in addition that God will make 'a covenant of peace' with Israel, 'an everlasting covenant', and will take up his dwelling among the people; and then the covenant formula follows in its two-term form (vv. 26f.). In 34.23ff. the installation of the new David is followed first by the covenant formula in version A (linked most unusually with the sovereignty of David, v. 24), and the text goes on to talk about the 'covenant of peace'. This has its special emphasis in its promise above all of a life of security and peace in the land after the return. In this

---

[6] See Section 6 of the present chapter.

respect this last text has its own profile in both domains, that of the covenant formula and that of *bᵉrît*.

Finally, the ceremony concluding a covenant in II Kings 11.17 must still be mentioned. Here too the *bᵉrît* which Jehoiada makes is closely connected with the covenant formula in version B, the formulation in which the substance of the covenant is said to be that Israel will be Yhwh's people. Despite the special character of this passage, it is further evidence for the close connection of the covenant formula and *bᵉrît*.

It emerges, then, that in a whole series of important passages the covenant formula and the term *bᵉrît* are closely interwoven. At the same time, we see that this is by no means a case of complete congruity, but that each of the two modes of expression can also be encountered without the other. In this respect we find here an important aspect of what was said at the beginning: that in defining the relationship of God and Israel more precisely, it is not useful to fix one's gaze one-sidedly on particular terms, since no one of them taken by itself expresses, or can express, the whole of that relationship. In Chapter IV we shall have to consider some consequences of the observations we have made in the present chapter.

3. *Covenant Formula and Exodus*

We already saw in Chapter III.1 that in the formulas introduced by להיות, 'in order to be', there is often a direct link with the deliverance from Egypt. This is also the case in other texts, and for that reason we shall look at these texts again here in their relation to each other.

In Ex. 6.6f. the two-term formula C appears as the final element in a series of declarations which begins with the phrase 'I will bring you out' (והוצאתי) and describes the impending liberation from Egypt in several stages. The establishment (or endorsement) of the mutual relationship of God and Israel is the goal to which the structure of these sentences points. Afterwards the divine speech begins again with the recognition formula, which once more begins with the declaration 'who brings you out' (המוציא). Thus in the complex fabric of this section of text the covenant formula is as it were framed by the double mention of the divine act of deliverance. In Lev. 26.12f. too, a text that corresponds to Exodus 6, the two-term covenant formula is followed by a self-utterance of Yhwh's, which begins with the words: 'who brought you out of the land of Egypt'.

Ex. 29.45f. is similar, covenant formula A here being followed by the recognition formula, which also continues with the words 'who brought you out'. In Lev. 22.32f. the sequence is reversed: the self-introductory formula is developed through the words 'who brings you out', and the covenant formula then follows. Lev. 25.38 reads almost identically, with only the syntactical change of the participle (המוציא) into a relative clause (אשר־הוצאתי). Lev. 26.45 is also similar. These latter examples particularly show the close, positively formula-like way in which the covenant formula is bound up with talk about the Exodus. This is all the more striking since in these cases the context gives little or no reason why the Exodus should be explicitly mentioned at all. Rather, through the antecedent 'in order to' of these instances, for Yhwh to be or to become Israel's God would actually appear to be the goal of the deliverance from Egypt.

In Deuteronomy too we twice find the link between the covenant formula and the Exodus. In Deut. 4.20 this link is as close as possible: the statement about the deliverance from Egypt flows directly into covenant formula B, which is again introduced by 'in order to', but here related to Israel's being a people for Yhwh. In 7.6ff. the declaration about the deliverance from Egypt is a component part of the reasoning which follows covenant formula B (v. 8); and it is significant that in this case the deliverance is viewed as Yhwh's performance of the oath he swore to the patriarchs. The fact that mention of the deliverance from Egypt is not a direct component of the formula here is made plain by the omission of any such mention from 14.2, where the wording is almost identical.

In II Samuel 7.23f. the covenant formula grows, as it were, out of the description of God's great acts for Israel, acts which culminate in the deliverance from Egypt.

In the book of Jeremiah the covenant formula is linked several times in a very marked way with the deliverance from Egypt. When God brought the Israelites out of their enslavement, what he required of them was not sacrifice but that they should listen to his voice—and then the covenant formula follows (7.22f.). Jer. 11.3f. is very similar; here, as in Dan. 7.8, a reminder of the divine oath to the patriarchs follows, an oath kept through the deliverance from Egypt (v. 5). In 31.32f., the promised 'new covenant' is contrasted with the earlier one, which God made with the forefathers when he brought them out of Egypt. The Israelites have broken the old covenant; consequently the new one is to be put into their hearts in such a way that it can no longer be broken. Here, therefore, a somewhat dubious light is shed on the deliverance from Egypt—not where God's act is concerned, but in respect of Israel's reaction. With this in mind we can understand 7.22f. too: at that time the Israelites did not understand what God's true and essential will was.

Thus these texts express in highly differing ways the conviction that God's relation to Israel, declared in the covenant formula, had its essential beginning in God's great act in liberating Israel from Egyptian bondage, an act, however, which embraced God's history with the patriarchs, to whom he had sworn to give the land.

4. *The Covenant Formula and Other Formulas*

We have seen that in a number of instances the covenant formula is linked more or less closely with other formula-like phraseology. This applies above all to two formulas which belong pre-eminently to Priestly language (including Ezekiel) and to which Zimmerli drew attention: the formula-like 'I am Yhwh' with its variants, which Zimmerli called the 'self-introductory formula',[7] and the 'recognition formula': 'They will/You will know (or shall know)',[8] which is not infrequently linked with the first. These formula-like elements are often used to structure texts, and it is interesting to see how in a series of passages the covenant formula has been incorporated into complex syntactical units of this kind. In many cases I can refer here to what I have already said, without any detailed recapitulation.

The section Ex. 6.2–8 offers a particularly striking example. The carefully structured text is divided up by three instances of the self-introductory formula 'I am Yhwh' (vv. 2b, 6a, 8b). In the second part, the covenant formula is at the centre, appearing here for the first time in its two-term form (v. 7a). It is taken further by way of the recognition formula, here in expanded form: 'You shall know that I am Yhwh, your God', which is then unpacked through the closer definition of the known God Yhwh as the one 'who brought you out of the slavery of the Egyptians'; and it ends, finally, with a repetition of the self-introductory formula. Here, in one of the central texts of Priestly Pentateuch theology, the covenant formula is a fixed element in the text's carefully wrought, theologically charged structure.

A similarly dense textual structure can be found in Ex. 29.45f. God announces that he will dwell in the midst of the Israelites; and what this means is defined more closely by way of covenant formula A: God dwells in the midst of the Israelites and by so doing shows himself to be Israel's God. This is carried forward through the declaration of recognition, which forms a transition to the announcement of the deliverance from Egypt; and at the end the self-introductory formula is repeated. Here again it is the two main formulas of Priestly language with which the covenant formula joins company.

In Lev. 11.44f., the covenant formula is a component in a complex sentence which is determined by the self-introductory formula. In its expanded form, 'For I am Yhwh, your God', it opens the whole passage. The first half is dominated by the theme of Israel's holiness, as a reflection of the holiness of Yhwh: 'You shall be holy for I am holy'. The second half then resumes with the short form of the

---

[7] See Chapter II, n. 23. We may leave on one side here the question whether the description is a particularly happy one. The formula was introduced into scholarly discussion under this name, and I am therefore using it here.

[8] See Chapter II, n. 24.

self-introductory formula with a prefatory כִּי: 'For I am Yhwh'. This is developed through the characterisation of Yhwh as the one 'who brought you out of Egypt', a declaration which is immediately followed by covenant formula A with לִהְיוֹת, 'in order to be'. The whole passage concludes in v. 45b with the word-for-word repetition of the sentence from v. 44aβ about the holiness of Israel and Yhwh. So here the covenant formula is interwoven with the themes of holiness and Exodus, and the whole is framed by the divine self-introductory formula.[9]

In Lev. 26.12f. the covenant formula is directly carried forward by the self-introductory formula, which here again is developed through the reference to the deliverance from Egypt. When the covenant formula (version A) recurs once more in v. 44f., it is embedded in a complex sentence which deals with God's 'remembrance' of his covenant. It is framed by the self-introductory formula, at the beginning in its expanded form with כִּי (v. 44b), at the end in the short form 'I am Yhwh'.

In Deut. 7.6–11 the covenant formula is part of a complex introductory sentence and is directly linked with the declaration of election. This is developed in a passage of argument about the divine reasons for the act of election, which passes over to the declaration of recognition (v. 9). The object of the recognition is to be 'that Yhwh himself [i.e. Yhwh alone] is God'.[10] This is unpacked by means of a number of epithets and closer characterisations of Yhwh, one of them being that he is also 'the keeper of the covenant'. Here, therefore, covenant formula, declaration of election, recognition formula and 'covenant' are closely and mutually related.

A quite specific relationship between covenant formula, declaration of recognition and self-introductory formula can be seen in Jer. 24.7. Equating the Judaeans in Babylonian exile with 'good figs', the verse says that God will give them a heart 'to know me, that I am Yhwh'; and this is then immediately followed by the covenant formula in its two-term form. What is striking about this fusing of the different fixed elements is that here the self-introductory formula appears in its 'pure' form, 'that I am Yhwh'; whereas otherwise when it is linked with the recognition formula it generally continues with a participial construction or a relative clause (cf., e.g., Ex. 6.7, 29.46).[11] Here, that is to say, it

---

[9] E. Blum drew attention to the importance of this passage in the context of the discussion of the 'Holiness Code'; see his *Studien zur Komposition des Pentateuch* (1990), 322f.

[10] On this see R. Rendtorff, '*El* als israelitische Gottesbezeichnung', *ZAW* 106 (1994), 19.

[11] W. Zimmerli, 'Erkenntnis Gottes nach dem Buche Ezekiel', AThANT 27 (1954), 34f. (= *Gottes Offenbarung* (1963), 73), also draws attention to the fact that here we have a doublet unique in the Hebrew Bible, since the text runs 'to know me, that I am Yhwh', whereas otherwise the form is either 'to know me' or 'to know that I am Yhwh'. Zimmerli assumes that this was deliberate, because the declaration 'that I am Yhwh' 'carries a particular emphasis which is not implicit in the mere accusative statement as it stands'.

is not a matter of knowing that Yhwh has done something in particular—that he has brought Israel out of Egypt, for example; the
knowledge is focused on Yhwh himself. This is the case in Jer.
31.31–34 too. Here as well the passage talks about Israel's hearts, into
which God will put the Torah; this is followed by the covenant formula,
and then by the statement that nobody will any longer teach anyone else
to 'know Yhwh', for everyone will know him (v. 34). The sequence of
the individual elements in chapter 31 differs from the sequence in
chapter 24; but in both cases the knowledge of Yhwh that comes from a
heart renewed by God is directly related to the bilateral covenant
formula. To stand in the relationship to God expressed through the
covenant formula means to know him.

Finally, in Ezek. 37.26ff. the link between the covenant formula and
the recognition formula appears yet once more under a different aspect.
God makes a 'covenant of peace' with Israel by taking up his dwelling
among the people, thereby establishing the relationship expressed in the
bilateral covenant formula. This will lead to *the peoples'* knowing 'that I
am Yhwh'. They will know that Yhwh is sanctifying Israel by setting up
his sanctuary among them. Here there are evident links with those texts
of the Priestly Pentateuch which talk about God's dwelling in the midst
of Israel,[12] as well as with passages there which say that God sanctifies
Israel through his own holiness.[13]

5. *The Covenant Formula in the Context of the Priestly Pentateuch*

It is in the Priestly Pentateuch that the covenant formula receives its
most profoundly reflected treatment. The formula appears at the essential key points of the account: in the first great divine speech to Abraham
in Genesis 17; in the communication of Yhwh's name and the
announcement of the decisive turn of events with the deliverance of
Israel from Egypt in Exodus 6; and at the end of the law-giving on Sinai
in Leviticus 26. On its first occurrence the formula appears in its simple
version A, announcing to Abraham and his descendants that Yhwh will
be their God (Gen. 17.7f.). It is then expanded to the full, two-term
formula C when God promises the Israelites that he will 'take' them to
be his people and will be their God (Ex. 6.7). And finally it appears
again in its two-term form, this time with its elements in reverse order:
God will dwell in the midst of Israel and will go with it into the
promised land, thus confirming his being God for Israel—a promise
which simultaneously includes the assurance that Israel is his people
(Lev. 26.12).

---

[12] Ex. 29.44f.; Lev. 26.11.
[13] Lev. 11.44f.

The covenant formula is at once the unfolding and the endorsement of the $b^e r \hat{\imath}t$, the covenant. In Gen. 17.7, Yhwh's being God for Israel is explicitly declared to be the substance of the 'everlasting covenant'. In Ex. 6.2–8 God calls to remembrance his covenant with the patriarchs (v. 4) and declares that he now 'remembers' his covenant (v. 5b) and will therefore bring Israel out of Egypt (v. 6), thus taking it to be his people and becoming its God (v. 7a). Lev. 26.9–13 reverts to this and expands the assurance embedded in the 'establishing of the covenant' about God's dwelling in the midst of Israel, which finds its objective in the covenant formula. At the end of the great chapter of blessing and curse, God once more acknowledges his $b^e r \hat{\imath}t$. He remembers the covenant (vv. 42, 45) and promises that, although the Israelites have broken it (v. 15), he himself will never break it (v. 44). We therefore see that at these key points in the Priestly Pentateuch conception, covenant formula and $b^e r \hat{\imath}t$ always appear together. They mutually interpret one another, so to speak.[14]

Another important element in the Priestly unfurling of the covenant formula is the link with other formulas characteristic of the Priestly tradition. In the exceedingly dense textual structure of Ex. 6.2–8, it is the self-introductory formula 'I am Yhwh' which first puts its stamp on the text (vv. 2, 6, 8). It provides the framework for $b^e r \hat{\imath}t$ and covenant formula, which appear here as essential elements of what God says about himself to Israel. These elements are joined by the recognition formula, which as third element adds to the making of the covenant and the mutual affiliation of God and Israel the deliverance from Egypt and the bringing into the promised land (vv. 7b, 8).

These Priestly formulas, however, also appear in connection with the covenant formula independently of the term $b^e r \hat{\imath}t$. Thus in Ex. 29.45f. recognition formula and self-introductory formula act as a way of unfolding the content of the covenant formula, so to speak. In addition, the recognition formula is again given concrete form through the deliverance from Egypt. In Lev. 11.44f. the self-introductory formula structures the passage in which covenant formula A about Yhwh's being God is set in a mutual relationship to Israel's being holy. The self-introductory formula appears twice, the second time filled out through a mention of the deliverance from Egypt (v. 45a). In Lev. 22.31–33 we encounter the self-introductory formula three times in the short form 'I am Yhwh'. The second time it introduces a passage which binds together in highly concentrated form several central theological statements: the sanctification of Israel, the deliverance from Egypt, and Yhwh's being God for Israel (vv. 32b, 33). Finally, in Lev. 25.23 and Num. 15.41 we find almost identical pronouncements, each of them introduced by the self-introductory formula, continuing with the

---

[14] On the consequences for $b^e r \hat{\imath}t$ see pp. 57f. below.

declaration about the deliverance from Egypt (in Lev. 25.23 with an additional statement about the gift of the land of Canaan), and ending with covenant formula A.

We therefore see that the covenant formula embraces all the essential themes and aspects of the theology of the Priestly composition of the Pentateuch. This is all summed up in most concentrated form in Ex. 6.2–8: Yhwh's self-introduction; the covenant theme; the 'remembrance' of the covenant as the turning point in Israel's destiny; the imminent deliverance from Egypt and the bringing into the land promised to the patriarchs; the recognition of God; and, at the centre, the covenant formula in its two-term form. All these aspects can also be encountered in varying concentration and in shifting combinations in the other passages in which the covenant formula appears. It is especially significant in this connection that the texts in Genesis 17 (as forerunner, so to speak), Exodus 6 and Leviticus 26 span the whole complex in a carefully crafted warp and weft of mutual cross-links, from God's first appearance to Abraham to the close of the law-giving on Sinai. There is no other theological formulation about which anything comparable could be said.

6. The Covenant Formula in the Context of Deuteronomy

In Deuteronomy the theological context in which the covenant formula appears is quite different. The special character of the theological conception already emerges from the circumstance that in Deuteronomy formula B (about Israel's being a people) is dominant, whereas the free-standing formula A about Yhwh's being God is missing entirely. This is in line with the fact that the statement about Israel's 'election' is a quite specific element in Deuteronomic theology. Here the covenant formula can act like a definition: God has chosen Israel to be his people (Deut. 7.6, 14.2). But the covenant formula is by no means to be found in all the passages in which the declaration about Israel's election occurs. It is missing in 4.37 and 10.14f., for example. On the other hand, we encounter the covenant formula at points where the word 'choose' is not used—for example in 4.20, 26.17f., 27.9, 28.9, 29.12. There is therefore a close relationship between these two ways of speaking, but they are not completely congruous.

It is remarkable, however, that the phrase עַם סְגֻלָּה, 'people of [his] possession', only appears in association with the covenant formula. 'To be a people for his possession' is accordingly a specific element in Deuteronomic theology. It appears in association with the word 'choose' in Deut. 7.6 and 14.2, as well as in the ceremony of commitment in 26.18. In 4.20 we find in addition the related expression עַם נַחֲלָה, 'people of [his] inheritance'. A glance at the concordance suggests that Ex. 19.5 should be included here too, since there the word 'possession' also follows the words 'you shall be for me'—admittedly, without the word 'people', but with the typically Deuteronomic phrase 'out of all peoples on earth'. These observations are important because they show that here a particular semantic field is closely bound up with the covenant formula.

The second important theme which is linked with the covenant formula in Deuteronomy is the deliverance from Egypt. In Deut. 4.20 the two are so closely interwoven that for Israel to be Yhwh's people appears as the actual purpose of the deliverance. It is hardly by chance that this is the first passage in Deuteronomy in which we encounter the covenant formula, and at the same time too the first passage which explicitly talks about the deliverance from Egypt. In addition, the initiating character of the Exodus event is very strongly stressed through the formulation that God has 'taken' Israel and brought it out of Egypt so that it might be his people. On the next occurrence of the covenant formula, in 7.6, the Exodus event also plays an important part, this time in association with typically Deuteronomic phraseology about Israel's 'election' by God. Here the deliverance appears to be the premise for the election, this time in a broader salvation-history context, with God's oath to the patriarchs (vv. 7f.). At the same time, it is clear that the link with the Exodus is determined by the context, for in 14.2, a text whose wording is almost identical with that of 7.6, the link is missing, because here the subject is quite different: Israel's 'holiness' over against the other peoples. In the other occurrences of the covenant formula in Deuteronomy there is no mention of the Exodus either.

One of Deuteronomy's central themes is the requirement that Israel keep God's commandments. This is linked with the covenant formula several times, and in different ways. The association is most direct in Deut. 27.9f., where the pronouncement 'Today you have become the people for Yhwh, your God' continues with the demand: 'You shall listen to the voice of Yhwh, your God, and keep his commandments and statutes that I am commanding you today'. Keeping the divine commandments is as it were the concrete form of Israel's adoption as God's people. In 28.9, the same connection is expressed in different terminology. The slightly varied covenant formula 'Yhwh will raise you up (הקים) for himself to be the holy people', with the coda 'as he has sworn to you', is followed by the statement (introduced by כי, 'for') 'You will keep the commandments of Yhwh, your God, and walk in his ways'.[15] Here again, the raising of Israel to be Yhwh's 'holy people' takes concrete form in the keeping of the commandments.

In Deut. 26.16–19 it is on the keeping of the commandments that

---

[15] Here the כי could stand as introduction to the following sentence: 'if you keep the commandments ... the peoples will see ...'

everything turns. In the build-up of this section of text, this requirement appears several times: in the introduction in an extensive double sentence (v. 16); in v. 17 as an explication of covenant formula A, that Yhwh will be Israel's God; and in v. 18 as explication of the corresponding covenant formula B, that Israel will be a people for Yhwh's possession. The term that links all three declarations is שמר, 'observe', 'keep' (vv. 16b, 17b, 18b). Both Yhwh's being God and Israel's being a people find their decisive expression in Israel's keeping of the commandments God has given. The whole finally issues in the declaration that God will raise Israel up above all peoples and will make it the 'holy people' (v. 19). Here therefore we find the concept of the 'holy people' and the keeping of the commandments related in the same way in the context of the covenant as in 28.9.

In the texts we have just considered, Deuteronomy 26, 27 and 28, it is noticeable that in none of the three do we find any of the other central themes of Old Testament tradition which can otherwise be linked with the covenant formula.[16] Conversely, it now emerges that in texts belonging to the first part of Deuteronomy the demand to keep the commandments is not presented in the same fundamental and all-inclusive way in connection with the covenant formula. If we look at the texts in the first parts of Deuteronomy, which like 26.19 and 28.9 talk about the 'holy people' in association with the covenant formula, it emerges that here the idea of Israel's divine election is dominant, and that therefore both in 7.6 and in 14.2 the context does not talk in general terms about fulfilling the commandments, but speaks very much more particularly about the cultic separation from the other peoples. In 7.11 it is then only at the end of an extensive section that the demand to keep the commandments is also formulated in general terms, whereas in chapter 14 there is no such generalisation.

Finally, the term *berît* also belongs to the context of the covenant formula in Deuteronomy. However, it is only in a single passage that the covenant formula is linked directly with the word *berît*, this also being the single occasion on which the formula appears in its bilateral form C: Deut. 29.11f. <12f.>. Here the text talks about the *berît* which Yhwh is making (כרת) with Israel, and then the covenant formula follows, introduced by למען: 'in order today to raise you up (הקים) to be a people for him, and he will be God for you'. The phrase 'in order to raise you up' is close to the more frequent להיות, 'in order to be'. Here, therefore, the covenant formula is linked with the term *berît* in such a way that the relationship between God and Israel which it expresses appears as the very substance of the *berît*. This relationship has its foundation in God's oath to the patriarchs (v. 12b).

---

[16] I am not entering more closely here into questions about the diachronic strata in Deuteronomy. But it is clear that in this respect the texts that follow the collection of laws in Deut. 12.2–26.15 display their own intention.

In chapters 4 and 7 the relation between the covenant formula and the word $b^e r\hat{\imath}t$ seems at first sight to be much less clear. The word $b^e r\hat{\imath}t$ is certainly used in each case in proximity to the covenant formula, 4.23 being close to 4.20 and 7.9 to 7.6. But the question is whether the two are related in the structure of the text, and if so, how. In chapter 4 the individual elements of this broadly laid-out theological chapter certainly cannot be separated from one another, so that a total theological cohesion emerges in which the two ($b^e r\hat{\imath}t$ and covenant formula) are related to one another. In chapter 7, v. 6 (in which the covenant formula appears) is followed by a passage of argument about the reason for Israel's election, which reaches its first climax in the statement that God is the 'upholder of the covenant' (v. 9). Here the relationship is clearer. Yet the connotation of the term $b^e r\hat{\imath}t$ differs in the two chapters, so that the broader connections can only become clear in a total theological interpretation.[17]

By and large, it emerges that, compared with the Priestly Pentateuch, the covenant formula has been employed less systematically in Deuteronomy. Thus it has no structuring function for the book as a whole, or for particular parts of it. At the same time, however, there are specific links with individual characteristic elements of Deuteronomic theology. This applies especially to the idea about Israel's election, and here again to Israel's description as a 'people for [God's] possession', which is always linked with the covenant formula. In 4.20, where the word 'choose' is missing (the expression 'take' being used instead), the purpose of the deliverance from Egypt is said to be that Israel should be the 'people of [God's] inheritance'. The idea is the same, but it is expressed in different terminology. Here too a close connection with the deliverance from Egypt is established, a connection which can also be found in 7.6 and 7.8, in less direct form. Thus the covenant formula embraces the thematic complex that God has chosen Israel and made it the people for his possession by bringing it out of Egypt. In the closing chapters of Deuteronomy the link between the covenant formula and the demand that the people keep the commandments is then especially marked, this demand once more being made in direct association with the term $b^e r\hat{\imath}t$ (29.11f.).

All in all we can see that in Deuteronomy the covenant formula is an important theological means of expression which can be linked with all the themes which are important for Deuteronomy's theology. At the same time, the way the formula is used varies greatly in different sectors of Deuteronomy, so that we get the impression that the covenant formula was one available means of expression parallel to others, and could be employed in different contexts with different functions in each particular case. Here two especially marked emphases can be

---

[17] See Chapter IV.2 below.

differentiated: in the first part the choosing of Israel to be the people for God's possession, and in the final chapters the demand that Israel keep the divine commandments.

7. The Covenant Formula in the Context of the Prophetic Books

In the prophets Jeremiah and Ezekiel[18] the covenant formula appears at salient points, and for the most part in salvation sayings, i.e. in the realm of expectation of the future. For an understanding of these sayings, however, it is significant that in Jeremiah, the first time the formula appears it is used in a different sense, in the context of the demand that the people listen to God's voice. In Jer. 7.23 this phrase is a summary expression for what God has expected from the Israelites ever since he brought them out of Egypt; and it is followed directly by the covenant formula. In 11.4 too the covenant formula follows the demand 'listen to my voice', which is given more precise form through 'and do all that I command you'. In the context, the expression 'my voice' (11.7) or 'my words' (11.10) alternates with the formulation 'words of this covenant' (11.2, 3, 6, 8), a phrase which constitutes the leitmotif of the section. Here, therefore, the covenant formula is closely linked with the expression *bᵉrît*, which in addition has the same connotation here as it has in Deuteronomy 26–28. In the contexts of both Jeremiah 7 and Jeremiah 11, the reproach to the Israelites that they have not listened to God's voice, or to the words of the covenant, stands at the centre.

The change in Jeremiah 24 is all the more impressive, the Judaeans in exile here being promised that God will bring them back from exile and will give them a heart to know him, and then the covenant formula follows—a new beginning which means at the same time a restoration of Israel's original condition. This is the consistent *cantus firmus* of all the succeeding texts in which the covenant formula appears in the book of Jeremiah; and the same may be said of those in the book of Ezekiel. The relationship between God and Israel is going to be restored on a new foundation. This is expressed in a particularly circumstantial and differentiated way in the announcement of the 'new covenant' in Jer. 31.31–34. The Israelites have broken the original covenant which God made with the patriarchs. They will no longer *be able* to break the new covenant, because God is putting it into their hearts. This promise is sealed through the covenant formula (v. 33b). In 32.38–40 the covenant formula introduces the promise of an 'everlasting covenant' which God is going to make with the inhabitants of restored Jerusalem and from which he will never depart. In Ezek. 37.26–28 the 'everlasting covenant' is also called a 'covenant of peace'; its foundation is said to be

---

[18] I am taking as my point of departure here the prophetic books as we have them, without discussing the question of the 'genuineness' of individual prophetic sayings.

God's dwelling in the midst of Israel, and it is endorsed by the covenant formula.

In the context of the prophetic books as a whole, the texts in which we encounter the covenant formula constitute no more than a limited part. But this part includes highly important theological statements, which are especially relevant to what talk about the 'covenant' means. We shall have to pursue this further in the next chapter.[19]

---

[19] With regard to the frequently discussed question whether there is an echo of the covenant formula in Hos. 1.9, it should be pointed out that the אהיה, 'I am', which has a central function there, frequently appears in the covenant formulas in the prophetic books: Jer. 11.4, 24.7, 30.22, 31.1, 32.38; Ezek. 11.20, 14.11, 34.24, 36.28, 37.23; Zech. 8.8.

IV

AN ATTEMPT AT A THEOLOGICAL SURVEY

Let us return to our starting point. The Hebrew Bible knows multifarious ways of expressing God's relationship to Israel. Especially striking examples of this are special terms, such as 'covenant' ($b^e r\hat{\imath}t$) and 'choose' (בחר), and stock phrases, such as the covenant formula, but also characteristic narrative or other texts which display no firmly fixed vocabulary of this kind. These various forms of expression can be found independently of one another in some texts, but they are often linked with each other as well. Here the covenant formula turns out to be a particularly important and characteristic linking element. This means that in many cases it is not particularly useful to look at the individual terms in isolation from each other, and that often this is not even possible.

In the past this isolated examination was applied especially often and intensively to the term $b^e r\hat{\imath}t$.[1] But our investigation, which started from the covenant formula, has shown that precisely this central term can also in many of its occurrences be understood differently and better if it is looked at in the relationships offered by its context. In the framework of our enquiry, we have by no means covered all instances of the word $b^e r\hat{\imath}t$, but nevertheless essential viewpoints about the position and function of this term in its different contexts have emerged. Above all, in this way of looking at things the question shifts. It is now no longer: what does the word $b^e r\hat{\imath}t$ mean in this passage?, or: what did the term mean 'originally'? The question is now: what statements are being made with this term, and with the terms and ideas associated with it, in this particular context?

The bond between 'covenant' and 'covenant formula' leads to a wider view of the relation between God and Israel. We have seen that, taken as a whole, the covenant formula is used very much more systematically than the term $b^e r\hat{\imath}t$. The main reason for this is that the covenant formula as such is an element in language moulded by theological reflection. Its very linguistic structure sets it firmly in syntactical cohesions in which what is stated in the formula itself is related to the content of other terms, formulas or facts. In the Pentateuch, it has in addition an overriding structuring function; and in this the term $b^e r\hat{\imath}t$ is included.

---

[1] Cf. E. W. Nicholson's summary and suggestive account, *God and his People: Covenant and Theology in the Old Testament* (1986); for new questions cf. now especially E. Zenger, 'Die Bundestheologie', in E. Zenger (ed.), *Der Neue Bund im Alten* (1993).

1. *Covenant Formula and Covenant in the Priestly Pentateuch*

The emphatic theological message at the beginning of the story of Abraham—which is to say at the beginning of Israel's history—is as follows: 'I am establishing my covenant between me and you and your descendants in their generations as an everlasting covenant: in order to be God for you and for your descendants after you' (Gen. 17.7). Yhwh is Israel's God for all time—that is the programmatic declaration about the substance of the covenant. This declaration is embedded in statements about other aspects of the covenant: God will multiply Abraham's descendants and will make of him a great people (vv. 2, 4, 6). God will give Abraham's 'offspring' the land of Canaan for an everlasting possession, thus endorsing his being God for Israel (v. 8). Corresponding to these divine declarations is the obligation laid upon Abraham to keep the covenant by circumcising all male descendants and members of their household (vv. 9–14). The circumcision is 'a sign of the covenant' (v. 11), which is again called an 'everlasting covenant' (v. 13). The person who violates this commandment is threatened with being 'cut off'—exterminated (v. 1).[2] Here we see the first beginnings of the covenant's bilateral character. On the one hand Abraham is entirely the recipient; but at the same time he has to observe the covenant through what he himself does. This obligation, however, like the punishment incumbent on failure to fulfil it, applies only to Abraham's individual descendants, not to the people of Israel as a whole. They are only mentioned later.

In the framework of the Pentateuch's composition, this detailed and differentiated definition of the covenant relationship between God and Israel also takes in the declaration of what, viewed diachronically,[3] is an earlier text stratum; this names as substance of the covenant only the promise of the land (Gen. 15.18–21). This should here above all be seen in a wider context, in association with other texts in which the deliverance from Egypt and the bringing into the land of Canaan are presented as being the fulfilment of the promise to the patriarchs (e.g. Ex. 32.11–13, 33.1). This can be said of Ex. 6.2–8 as well. To look back to the covenant with the patriarchs puts the promise of the land in the foreground (v. 4), and 'remembrance' of the covenant leads to the consequence that God will bring Israel out of the bondage in Egypt (vv. 5b, 6). It is only here and now that Israel is accepted by God as a 'people', which is why it has been in Egypt. This is the full exposition of the covenant, the foundation for which began with Abraham (Gen. 17.7). The close connection between the (from now on completely

---

[2] Cf. R. Rendtorff, 'Die sündige næfæš', in *Was ist der Mensch ...? Festschrift H.-W. Wolff* (1992), 213.

[3] The diachronic strata of the Pentateuch texts will be taken into consideration in what follows, but the texts will be read as they now stand.

bilateral) relationship between God and Israel on the one hand, and the deliverance from Egypt with the bringing into the land promised to the patriarchs on the other, is again disclosed in the recognition formula (vv. 7b, 8).

A new chapter in the history of the covenant between God and Israel begins with Israel's arrival at Sinai. In the first divine speech on Sinai, God pronounces Israel to be his 'possession out of all the peoples', the proviso being that 'they listen to my voice and keep my covenant' (Ex. 19.5). Here Israel's relationship to God as it is defined in the terminology of the covenant formula is related to the covenant in such a way that the requirement to Abraham 'to keep' the covenant is now extended to Israel as a whole. In addition the 'keeping of the covenant' is not now concentrated on one particular point, as it was in the case of Abraham, with the circumcision; it is extended to 'listening to my voice'. This formulation proleptically denotes the commandments and precepts which God is going to proclaim in what follows. In v. 8, and then again in 24.3 and 7, we are told Israel's answer: 'We will do (and listen)'. With this the covenant is constituted. The proviso contained in the כִּי, 'if', in 19.5 has basically been fulfilled.

God intensifies his commitment to Israel even further by resolving 'to dwell in the midst of the Israelites' (Ex. 29.45f.). This will be a renewed confirmation that he is Israel's God. The building of the sanctuary with which Moses is charged is to be the visible sign of this. At the same time its aim is to bring about the recognition among the Israelites that God has brought them out of Egypt for the very purpose of dwelling among them.

And yet the covenant is soon afterwards endangered through Israel's apostasy with the Golden Calf. In Moses's dramatic struggle with God this danger is surmounted. God resolves that even though Israel is 'stiff-necked' (Ex. 32.9, 34.9) he will make (כרת) the covenant afresh (34.10). The rest of the story shows that God stands by his covenant and adheres to it. He is שֹׁמֵר הַבְּרִית וְהַחֶסֶד, 'keeper of the covenant and of grace', as later passages say (Deut. 7.9; Neh. 9.32). Here, therefore, at the beginning of the history of the covenant, we can discern the enormous tension to which the relationship between God and Israel is subject: God has made, or 'established', his covenant with Israel; Israel has declared itself prepared to fulfil the obligation arising out of this covenant relationship to keep the divine commandments; but Israel has proved a failure, and has broken the covenant on its side; yet for all that God stands fast by his covenant, quite apart from anything that Israel will still do, 'stiff-necked' as it is. At the very beginning of the history of the covenant between God and Israel, this makes the fundamental experiences and decisions plain. Israel has broken the covenant and now no longer lives in a state of 'innocence' in the covenant that was originally concluded. Instead it lives in the covenant which God has re-established, and which is now guaranteed solely through God's grace.[4]

On several other occasions light is thrown from different angles on the covenant relationship between God and Israel. Israel's 'holiness', conferred by God, is a further purpose of the deliverance from Egypt. Yhwh's being God for Israel and Israel's holiness 'because I am holy' are meant to correspond to each other (Lev. 11.44f.). Lev. 22.31–33 speaks very similarly, adding the requirement to keep the commandments. Lev. 25.38 stresses yet again the gift of the land to the Israelites as an expression of Yhwh's being God for Israel.

And yet, for all that, the tension existing ever since Israel's sin with the Golden Calf has by no means disappeared from the awareness of the biblical authors. In Leviticus 26, at the end of the law-giving on Sinai, a scenario is developed to show what can happen to Israel. In the first section (vv. 3–13) the positive aspects of life in obedience to the covenant are described. Israel will enjoy abundant blessing and peace; God will 'establish' his covenant and will dwell in Israel's midst; he will be their God, and they will be his people, for he has brought them as free men and women out of Egypt. But then, with the words 'But if you do not listen to me', a long dismaying description follows of what will happen to Israel if it violates its covenant obedience (vv. 14–39). Yet at the end the turn of events is after all on the horizon, so that God finally once more remembers his covenant (v. 40) and promises that he will never break it (v. 44), and he remembers the covenant with the earlier generation whom he brought out of Egypt 'in order to be God for them' (v. 45).

Here the wheel that began turning in Genesis 17 comes full circle: Yhwh is Israel's God—that is and remains the decisive content of the covenant. Everything else takes its significance from that and points to that. This is already true first of the second part of the covenant formula (formula B), which in fact never appears by itself in the Priestly Pentateuch. It is solemnly and formally introduced in Exodus 6 after Yhwh has first again remembered the covenant made with Abraham (v. 6), in which he declared his being God for Israel to be the real substance of the covenant. Now, however, he stresses another element in the covenant assurance of Genesis 17: the promise of the land. He now picks this up by taking Abraham's descendants 'to be his people', in order for them and with them to fulfil the promise given to Abraham.

Here another central element now emerges, one which is closely linked with the declaration about Yhwh's being God for Israel: the deliverance from Egypt. We have already seen that parallel to, or after, Exodus 6 in particular, formula A, 'to be God for you', is always linked

[4] Cf. here Rendtorff, '"Covenant" as a Structuring Concept in Genesis and Exodus', in *Canon and Theology* (ET 1993), 129ff.; C. Dohmen, 'Der Sinaibund als Neuer Bund nach Ex 19–34', in Zenger (ed.), *Der Neue Bund im Alten*, 51–83.

in the Priestly Pentateuch with the deliverance from Egypt.[5] At the same time, however, it also became plain that this is not just a formula-like mention of this act of God's; it has a particular emphasis in each of the passages where it occurs. Thus in Lev. 11.45 the wording is: 'For I am Yhwh, who has brought you out of the land of Egypt, in order to be God for you; and you shall be holy, for I am holy' (cf. also Lev. 22.32f. and Num. 15.41). Yhwh's being God for Israel is to be reflected in the holiness of the people who have been liberated from Egypt. In Lev. 25.38 the double purpose of the deliverance is also expressed even more tersely through the double ל, 'in order to': 'I am Yhwh your God, who brought you out of the land of Egypt in order to give you the land of Canaan, in order to be God for you'. God will be Israel's God in the land he gives them. In the context of Leviticus 25, however, this means that the land belongs to Yhwh himself (v. 23). In Lev. 26.45 we are told that God remembers his covenant with the earlier generations 'whom I brought out of the land of Egypt before the eyes of the peoples, in order to be God for them. I am Yhwh.' So now too God's renewed commitment to Israel is to prove his power 'before the eyes of the peoples'. Finally, in Ex. 29.45, in a somewhat different linguistic formulation, God's dwelling in the midst of Israel is linked with his being God and with the deliverance from Egypt. Here the covenant formula is additionally followed by the recognition formula: 'And they shall know that I am Yhwh, their God, who brought them out of the land of Egypt in order to dwell in their midst. I am Yhwh, their God.' The presence of God in the midst of his people is one of the essential goals of the deliverance from Egypt.

If we again extend the arc still further and draw in the most important passages dealing with God's covenant with Israel, which in conjunction with the covenant formula present the Pentateuch's picture of the history of the covenant, then at every point we find the reference to the deliverance from Egypt. On the arrival at Sinai, God's first address to Israel begins with the words: 'You have seen what I did to the Egyptians' (Ex. 19.4). The phrase ועתה, 'and now', marks the transition from the Exodus to Sinai and thus to the covenant (v. 5). In the dramatic events and discussions about the endangering of the covenant through the Golden Calf in Exodus 32–34, the deliverance from Egypt is at the centre: on the one hand as God's act, carried out by Moses, which the Israelites now hold cheap (God to Moses: 'your people, whom you brought up out of the land of Egypt', 32.7), and on the other hand as the act about which Moses reminds God ('your people, whom you brought out of the land of Egypt with great power and with a mighty hand', v. 11). And finally, it is not just the end of the great chapter 26 of Leviticus

---

[5] Of course this does not apply to Genesis 17, where the formula 'in order to be God for you' is addressed to Abraham.

that speaks of the deliverance from Egypt.[6] It is mentioned at the beginning too, in the confirmation of the covenant (v. 13).

All this could now prompt the question: when did God then 'make' the covenant, and with whom? There have been a number of attempts to decide this question in one sense or another and to derive, or justify, different theological positions from the answer.[7] Here we must first be clear that in the context of the Priestly Pentateuch there is no doubt at all that Abraham was the first recipient of the divine promise of a covenant. This cannot be called in question even by the different emphases given in texts that followed later. In addition, utterances about the covenant formula repeatedly relate the deliverance from Egypt expressly to the patriarchs Abraham, Isaac and Jacob (e.g., Ex. 6.4f.; Lev. 26.42–45). But we shall come back to this in more detail later.[8]

2. Covenant Formula, Covenant and Election in Deuteronomy

The initial situation in Deuteronomy is fundamentally different from that of the previous books of the Pentateuch. The first great periods of Israel's history belong to the past: the generation of the patriarchs, to whom the land was promised, as Moses reminds the people in the first sentences of his speech in Deuteronomy (1.8); the deliverance from Egypt, which has a constitutive function in several ways for the present situation and for Israel's self-understanding (4.20, 7.8 and passim); the foundational events at Horeb (= Sinai), where God swears Israel into his 'covenant' (4.9–14); the journey through the desert, the abortive attempt to conquer the country from Kadesh, the forty years' wandering in the wilderness, the conquest of the kings east of the Jordan and the occupation of their country (1.19–3.17), down to the point 'beyond the Jordan in the land of Moab' (1.5) where Moses now begins his summary exposition of the law.

Everything that has led up to this point is the object of backward-looking reflection. In the framework of our present subject, this may be said particularly about God's commitment to Israel, which is constitutive for the covenant. This commitment is presupposed as datum. That best explains why in Deuteronomy the covenant formula regularly appears in the form of formula B, 'to be a people for him'. The other side of the covenant formula, that Yhwh is Israel's God, is one of the

---

[6] See the discussion above on Lev. 26.45.

[7] W. Zimmerli did this in most pronounced fashion with his thesis that the Priestly Writing 'ruthlessly pushed out' the tradition about the making of the covenant at Sinai, and spoke only of a covenant made by God with Abraham; see Zimmerli, 'Sinaibund und Abrahambund: Ein Beitrag zum Verständnis der Priesterschrift', *ThZ* 16 (1960), 268–280; reprinted in *Gottes Offenbarung* (1963), 205–216.

[8] See Section 4 of the present chapter.

undisputed, and hence also undiscussed, premises for the self-understanding of Israel which is the basis here. In the present Pentateuchal context, Deuteronomy in this way picks up the thread of the previous books and expounds the covenant formula further in a special sense.

In this connection, the consequences which emerge for Israel from the fact that Yhwh is Israel's God are the main point. This becomes quite clear at the first instance of formula B, in Deut. 4.20. Here Israel's encounter with other peoples is presupposed, although in actual fact this only came about after the occupation of the land. Deuteronomy 4 makes this caesura very clearly: the commandments which Moses passes on to the Israelites are to be kept 'in the land that you are about to enter and occupy' (v. 5). That means immediate confrontation with other peoples, from whom Israel is to keep apart (vv. 6ff.). In this connection the passage goes on to say in extremely pointed form that God has 'taken' the Israelites precisely for this purpose and has brought them out of Egypt in order that they should not behave like other peoples and worship other gods, but so that 'you should become a people for his inheritance' (v. 20). God has 'chosen' Israel (v. 37) and consequently 'You shall acknowledge today and take to heart that Yhwh is God in heaven above and on the earth beneath; there is no other' (v. 39). Here the recognition formula introduces the declaration that Yhwh is higher and greater even than the constellations which he has allotted to the other peoples as object of worship (v. 19).

In the context of Deuteronomy 4,[9] therefore, the covenant formula stands in a clear mutual relationship to the term 'choose' (בחר). But the word 'covenant' (ברית) is also mentioned in this context, and it appears here for the first time in Deuteronomy. Looking back to the day when Israel stood before God at Horeb (v. 10f.), the passage says: 'He declared to you his covenant which he charged you to observe, that is the Ten Words, and he wrote them on two stone tablets' (v. 13). In v. 23 Israel is again exhorted not to forget the covenant; and here the covenant is explicated through the prohibition of images. Finally, v. 31 says that God himself 'will not forget the covenant with your forefathers that he swore to them'. These multiple variations on the covenant theme belong together here with both the covenant formula and Israel's 'election'. God 'swore' a covenant to the patriarchs, filled it with content on Horeb, and admonishes Israel not to forget it—just as he will not forget it either (vv. 23 and 31 use the verb שכח, 'forget', both times). It is obvious here that the word *berît* in v. 31 points to God's oath to the patriarchs, who were already mentioned in 1.8: the oath swearing to bring them and their descendants into 'the promised land'.[10] But these are not two different

[9] See N. Lohfink, 'Verkündigung des Hauptgebots in Dt 4,1–40', *Bibel und Leben* 5 (1964); revised version in 'Höre Israel!' (1965; reprinted in *Studien zum Deut.* 1 (1990), 167–191).

[10] Lohfink, *Die Väter Israels im Deuteronomium* (1991), 59.

covenants.[11] Rather, they are linked through the 'not forgetting' on both sides. We shall come back to this again later.

In Deuteronomy 7 Israel's relationship to the other peoples again moves into the centre. Here everything turns on the extremely pregnant v. 6, where three elements of theological tradition are fused into a unity: (1) Israel is a 'holy people' (עם קדוש) for Yhwh; (2) Yhwh has 'chosen [Israel] out of all peoples'; (3) Israel is to be 'a people for him'. This last covenant formula is expanded here into 'to be a people for his possession' (לעם סגלה). It forms the crystallisation point for the declarations grouped round it.

The first section of the chapter (vv. 1ff.) gravitates, as it were, towards v. 6. Israel is to surrender to destruction the peoples whom God is going to deliver into its hand. Above all, Israel is not to make any contract (כרת ברית) with them or enter into any marriages, for these things involve the danger of being seduced into the worship of other gods. Consequently the altars and cultic objects of these peoples are to be destroyed. Israel has been chosen by God to be his holy people and a people for his own possession; and that makes this demarcation line between Israel and the other peoples necessary.[12]

With v. 7 another line of argument begins, set in motion, as it were, by v. 6. Why has God chosen Israel? The answer begins with a negative: not because of Israel's own greatness. Then a highly concentrated text follows in which different elements of tradition are interlaced (v. 8). God loved Israel. That is why he kept the oath which he swore to the patriarchs and, with a strong arm, has brought Israel out of slavery, out of the hand of Pharaoh, and has redeemed it. In this context the 'oath' which the text talks about stands in direct proximity to the 'covenant', whose upholder God is said to be (v. 9). For through God's faithfulness to his oath, which he proved in the deliverance from Egypt, Israel is to 'know' that God is the dependable God, who keeps his covenant and remains faithful.[13]

Then the connotation of the word *bᵉrît* shifts. God keeps his covenant and remains loyal to the people who keep his commandments. This is further developed into an explicit exhortation to keep the commandments (v. 11). The 'keeping' (שמר) of the commandments on Israel's side corresponds to God's 'keeping' of the covenant and the faithfulness towards Israel 'which he swore to your forefathers' (v. 12). This is then

---

[11] Thus Lohfink, *Die Väter Israels*, 60. But see Section 4 of the present chapter.

[12] I cannot discuss here the problems involved in these directives to destroy other peoples. But in my view the very trend of Deut. 7.1–6 shows that this is meant essentially, if not exclusively, as a religious demarcation. There is, in my opinion, no historical reality underlying the assertions of destruction which are associated with this in Deuteronomy.

[13] On the terminology and on Deuteronomy 7 as a whole, see Lohfink, 'Bundestheologie im Alten Testament: Zum gleichnamigen Buch von L. Perlitt' (1973; reprinted in *Studien zum Deut.* 1 (1990), 342ff.).

followed by a broadly laid-out presentation of the blessing which God will confer on obedient Israel. As already in chapter 4, therefore, God's 'covenant' takes in both aspects: the oath to the forefathers, which God will implement when he brings Israel into 'the land', and the covenant which acquired its concrete form at Horeb, in the divine commandments. This characteristic intermediate position assumed by the word *bᵉrît* is intensified still more by the link with the word חסד, *ḥesed* (vv. 9 and 12), which can be rendered here as 'faithfulness'. This link looks like a formula, and we meet it again a number of times in various Old Testament writings.[14] But in Deuteronomy it is used only here. It is interesting in this connection to see how in v. 9 the emphasis shifts in what the declaration of recognition says. First of all it runs, as it did in 4.35 and 39: 'You shall know that Yhwh your God (alone) is God'. But this confessional formulation[15] is expanded by way of another formula-like phrase: 'the dependable God, who keeps the covenant and remains faithful'. This phrase is closely related to similar formulations found in several of the instances already cited where the words *bᵉrît* and *ḥesed* are paired: Dan. 9.4; Neh. 1.5, 9.32. These complex declarations are not simply and solely an admonition to keep the commandments: this has already been made clear through their introduction with the recognition pronouncement in v. 9, where the 'knowing' is supposed to be gained from the fact of Israel's deliverance and 'redemption' from Egypt. This is underlined even more by the phrase 'as he swore to your forefathers', which is used twice (vv. 8 and 12).

Here, therefore, different aspects of the term *bᵉrît* stand side by side in the context, and are related to each other and interwoven in a number of ways. It does not seem particularly useful to try to allot these different aspects to different 'covenants', and then to draw literary-critical conclusions from the result—or, conversely, to try to underpin the distinction with the help of literary-critical criteria. The text of Deuteronomy as we now have it apparently uses this word as one term—but not the only one!—with which to express the relationship between God and Israel, and in this term various different aspects of that relationship are reflected. If we do not just look at the word *bᵉrît* in isolation, but see it in context with the covenant formula, for example, and also with the concept of 'election', and if we follow up the wider connections which then emerge, the different aspects lose their seemingly divisive character. Instead they reflect the different facets of God's relationship to Israel, which in Deuteronomy as a whole finds expression in manifold ways. That God gave to the patriarchs the promise of the land, sealing the promise with an oath; that he brought the later generation out of Egypt in performance of this oath, and chose them to be 'a people for his

---

[14] I Kings 8.23 (II Chron. 6.14); Dan. 9.4; Neh. 1.5, 9.32.
[15] Cf. Rendtorff, ''*El* als israelitische Gottesbezeichnung', *ZAW* 106 (1994), 19.

own possession'; that at Horeb he bound Israel to keep his commandments; and that he is about to put the final seal on all this by bringing
Israel into the promised land—this great complex is not rendered by any
one term, but is expressed in a number of fixed terms and phrases, which
can also be linked with each other again and again. Among these words
and phrases, the term $b^e r \hat{i} t$ undoubtedly has the most clearly defined
profile—not least because of the Jewish and Christian interpretative
tradition, among other things. But on its first occurrence in chapter 4 the
word is used as one familiar expression parallel to others. And in
26.16–19, where the relationship between God and Israel is sealed in a
solemn ceremony, the term is missing altogether.

The theological discussions in the introductory chapters of Deuteronomy—especially chapters 4 and 7—which reach back to the past find
hardly any echo in the body of the law (Deut. 12–26.15). We only
encounter the covenant formula once, in 14.2. This sentence is almost
identical with 7.6, but it has a completely different function, developing
the meaning of Israel's 'holiness' on the basis of the distinction between
clean and unclean animals. And here the covenant formula stands by
itself, without any link with other theological termini or formulas. But
its use at this point shows that it was available as a specific expression
for the relationship between God and Israel. Incidentally, we also come
across the word $b^e r \hat{i} t$ once only in the body of the law, in the description
of a hypothetical case of infringement of the first commandment, which
is described as 'transgressing the $b^e r \hat{i} t$' (17.2). This word too appears
here in a rather isolated position.[16]

At the end of the body of the law comes the solemn scene of mutual
commitment between God and Israel (Deut. 26.16–19). The most remarkable thing about this in our present context is that here for the first time in
Deuteronomy it is not only the second part of the covenant formula
(formula B) which appears (in which Israel is called God's people)—this
is preceded by the first part (formula A), which talks about Yhwh's being
God for Israel. But this is also the only occasion in the Hebrew Bible when
this bilateral declaration is not made in a single sentence (formula C), but
in two separate statements, each with its own context. Finally, this is the
one passage in which Israel itself is introduced as speaker. In all other
cases (with the exception of II Kings 11.17; see below) the לְהְיוֹת, 'in order
to be', is a declaration about the consequence or implication of a divine
act: God has brought Israel out of Egypt (Deut. 4.20); or chosen it (7.6,
14.2) so that it might be his people; or he has 'taken' Israel to be his people
(Ex. 6.7); etc. In Deuteronomy 26, Israel says that it desires to be God's
people—or, according to another interpretation, that Yhwh is its God.[17]

---

[16] Lohfink, 'Die Sicherung der Wirksamkeit des Gotteswortes', *Studien zum Deut.* 1
(1990), 320, misses the word 'Torah' here. Apparently the word $b^e r \hat{i} t$ fulfils its function at
this point.

[17] See Chapter II, n. 43, above.

(Only II Kings 11.17 is comparable, where the content of the covenant made by King Jehoiada is said to be 'that they should be a people for Yhwh', which is in substance a declaration on Israel's part.)

The more we enter into the structures of the covenant formula(s) and their respective contexts, the clearer the special position of the ceremony in Deuteronomy 26 becomes. It was initially taken as the starting point for investigations of the 'covenant formula' mainly because of the presumption that it could be connected with the covenant made by Josiah, which is reported in II Kings 23.1–3. If this were the case, one *Sitz im Leben* for the covenant formula—or perhaps even the original one—would have been discovered. But however convincing the relationship between these two texts may seem to be at first sight, a number of serious differences remain. The most important seems to me to be that in II Kings 23.3 it is not even the mutual commitment which is expressed, i.e. there is no mention of Yhwh's being God for Israel. So what constitutes the special feature of Deut. 26.16–19 within Deuteronomy as a whole is missing in II Kings 23. Indeed, in II Kings 23 there is no covenant formula at all, 'nor is there any reference to it in any recognisable form'.[18] Conversely, in II Kings 23.3 the word $b^e r\hat{\imath} t$ is used at a central point, highly emphasised in addition through the use of the definite article: 'The king ... made the covenant before Yhwh'. In Deuteronomy 26, on the other hand, the word $b^e r\hat{\imath} t$ is missing.

In the context of Deuteronomy this ceremony of commitment stands at a highly prominent point, at the end of the great discourse which begins in chapter 12, in which Moses passes on to the Israelites the 'statutes and ordinances' which God has given them and which they are to keep. Deut. 26.16 looks back to 12.1, and the commitment ceremony then follows. Here its function seems quite clear. It puts the seal, as it were, on what Moses has expounded in his speech to the Israelites. Yhwh is God for Israel: this has been the presupposition from the very beginning for everything said in Deuteronomy; that is why there has hitherto been no need to pronounce the first part of the covenant formula explicitly. It was continually present whenever there was a mention of God's acts for Israel, especially the deliverance from Egypt, which was a continually reiterated theme. Even if God 'chose' Israel, declaring it to be 'a holy people' and 'a people for his own possession', all this was only possible, after all, because he was Israel's God. And if Israel 'knew' that Yhwh alone is God (4.35, 39; 7.9), then this 'knowing' came about in the context of his acts on Israel's behalf. In this respect the first part of the covenant formula does not introduce anything new here, but makes explicit the presupposition for everything that has been said up to now.

In Deuteronomy up to this point, the covenant formula has usually been a component in a more extensive syntactical unit; but in Deuteronomy 26

---

[18] Lohfink, 'Dt 26,17–19 und die "Bundesformel"', in *Studien zum Deut.* 1 (1990), 254.

the important thing is evidently the *separate* emphasis of the two formulas formed with ...לְ ...לְ, לִהְיוֹת, 'in order to be for ... for ...'. Whatever answer is found for the difficult syntactical question, the statements of the two corresponding formulas are unmistakable and are in line with the way they are used elsewhere: 'to be God for you' (v. 17)—'to be a people for his own possession' (v. 18). One special feature, however, is that both formulas are related to Israel's keeping of the commandments: because Yhwh is Israel's God, Israel will walk in his ways (v. 17); and because Israel is the people for Yhwh's possession, it will keep his command- ments. It becomes evident here that the special structure of this two-part covenant formula is determined by its position and function at the end of the great proclamation of the law. Nowhere else is the covenant formula in its two-element form so clearly focused—indeed to an almost one-sided degree—on Israel's observance of the divine commandments.

Concentration on the keeping of the commandments can also be found in the two following passages with formula B, however. (1) In Deut. 27.9f., this is the only declaration which gives the covenant formula more precise form: to listen to God's voice and fulfil his commandments. (2) In 28.9 the horizon of the statement is spread a little more widely, inasmuch as the text speaks of Israel's being raised up to be 'a holy people', supplementing this by a reference to the past: 'as he [Yhwh] swore to you'. But these statements hardly have an independent function, compa- rable, for example, with the instances in chapters 4 and 7. Here, rather, the covenant formula is at the service of the call to observe the divine commandments, which dominates these chapters following the preaching of the law. They are therefore an element in which the weight in Deuter- onomy shifts from the historical and parenetic introductory chapters to the frequently varied requirement to fulfil the divine commandments.

Towards the end of Deuteronomy, the covenant formula appears once more, in 29.12 <13>. This is the only occasion in Deuteronomy when the bilateral formula C is used in its 'normal' form, i.e. in a single sentence. Its context in vv. 9–14 suggests that something is being 'put on record'— perhaps a cultic covenant ceremony with the covenant formula at its centre.[19] This central position is now also important for the formula's function in the context of Deuteronomy as a whole. Here the formula is expressly introduced by לְמַעַן, 'in order to', as the explication of the immediately preceding declaration that God is making a covenant with the assembled people. He is making this covenant 'today'; that is stated five times in this section. And he is making it as he promised the generation now being addressed he would do, and as he had already sworn before that to their forefathers Abraham, Isaac and Jacob. The substance of the covenant is that 'today' God is raising Israel up to be a people, and that he himself will be Israel's God. This declaration is given an immensely

---

[19] Lohfink, 'Der Bundeschluß im Land Moab', in *Studien zum Deut.* 1 (1990), 61 and 66.

weighty position at the beginning of the great discourse Deuteronomy 29–30 (with its introduction in 28.69 <29.1>). In the framework of Deuteronomy as a whole, this means that the direct mutual relationship between God and Israel which has already been expressed at a number of prominent points in the Priestly Pentateuch is valid for Deuteronomy too, in spite of the fact that here in specific instances the importance of this relationship for Israel itself is given the greater stress. In 29.12 <13> the formula dominant in Deuteronomy—formula B—which speaks of Israel as God's people, flows, as it were, into the great, complete formula C; for this, 26.16–19 has already prepared the ground.

Here we can now note a point which has significance for the Pentateuch as a whole. It is only twice that the covenant formula appears as a direct explication of $b^e r \hat{\imath} t$, 'covenant': at its first occurrence, in Gen. 17.7, and at its last, in Deut. 29.12 <13>. The first time it is only formula A, in which God promises Abraham that he will be his God; the second time it is the bilateral formula C, in which, once again and in conclusion, the mutual relationship between God and Israel is endorsed, the relationship which is determinative for the whole of the Pentateuch. Here too the bridge is formed by Exodus 6, which says that God remembers the covenant with the patriarchs (vv. 4f.) and is for that reason 'taking' their descendants to be his people. The terminology in the two passages (or in all three) differs. In Genesis 17 God 'establishes' (הקים) the covenant (thus also Ex. 6.4); in Deuteronomy 29 he 'makes' it (כרת, v. 11 <12>). Deuteronomy 29 instead uses the word הקים, 'establish', for Israel's installation as God's people (as earlier in 28.9 too). These differences reflect the diachronic strata of the texts. But precisely in so doing they also confirm that on the level of the Pentateuch's final form (or its composition) they are meant to be read in their relation to each other. God's covenant with Israel, interpreted through the covenant formula, spans and moulds the first foundational epoch of Israel's history as this is reflected in the Pentateuch.

3. The Covenant Formula and 'the New Covenant' in the Prophets

In the prophetic books the covenant formula appears late. This corresponds to the occurrence of the term $b^e r \hat{\imath} t$, which is missing in the early prophetic books,[20] and also to the use of the term 'choose', which is an established term in the language of Deuteronomy. This already indicates that in the books of the Hebrew Bible, systematic theological reflection only emerges at all clearly in the Deuteronomic period.[21] The question

---

[20] L. Perlitt uses for this the often approvingly quoted phrase '"silence about the covenant" among the eighth-century prophets'; see his *Bundestheologie im Alten Testament* (1969), 129ff.

[21] Cf. among others S. Herrmann, 'Die konstruktive Restauration: Das Deuteronomium als Mitte biblischer Theologie', in *Probleme biblischer Theologie: Festschrift G. von Rad* (1971), 155–170 (reprinted in *Gesammelte Studien* (1986), 163–178).

about priorities and dependencies need not concern us here. Instead, our purpose is rather to trace the theological meaning and function of the covenant formula in the prophetic books in which the formula appears.

In the book of Jeremiah we first encounter the covenant formula linked with phraseology where we can hear echoes of formulations in the Pentateuch, in Deuteronomy in particular. When God brought the forefathers out of Egypt, he gave them the commandment: 'Listen to my voice, then I will be your God and you shall be my people' (Jer. 7.23). Jer. 11.4 is similar, the reminder of the deliverance from Egypt and the phrase 'listen to my voice' preceding the covenant formula there too. If we look more closely, however, we can see that in this instance two declarations are linked which in Deuteronomy are never found together. In Deuteronomy, the reminder of the deliverance from Egypt has the function of stressing God's saving acts on Israel's behalf (Deut. 4.20, 7.8), whereas the exhortation to listen to God's voice is found in completely different contexts (Deut. 13.19 <18>, 15.5 and frequently elsewhere). But Jer. 7.21–24 is concerned with the question of what God commanded the Israelites when he brought them out of Egypt: not sacrifice but that they should listen to God's voice; it is only after this that the covenant formula is added. The deliverance from Egypt remains God's saving act for Israel, but it is at the same time the point at which God began to give Israel his commandments.

The interweaving of these two aspects is clearer still in Jer. 11.3–5. In an extended syntactical unit, the keeping of the 'covenant' which God commanded of the forefathers when he brought them out of Egypt is first of all emphatically inculcated, and what God has said is quoted, as in 7.23: 'Listen to my voice and do all that I command you'; and this is again followed by the covenant formula. But then the aspect of the deliverance in the context of salvation history is stressed: 'that I may perform the oath that I swore to your forefathers, to give them a land flowing with milk and honey, as at this day'. Here two generations of ancestors are being talked about, but from the viewpoint of the generation now addressed they move into close proximity to each other, as recipients of God's promises and his salvific acts in the early era.[22] It is important in this connection that Jeremiah by no means allows the salvation-history aspect to be forgotten, or to give way entirely to a stress on the divine commandments.

In these two texts, the covenant formula is presented under a new aspect. God has bound his relationship to Israel as it is expressed in the bilateral formula to the 'listening to his voice'—that is, to the keeping of his commandments. This viewpoint appears here in the form of prophetic criticism of the failure of the Israelites addressed to fulfil this

[22] I shall not enter here into the dispute between Römer and Lohfink about this question, but see T. Römer, *Israels Väter* (1990), 422ff., and Lohfink, *Die Väter Israels*, 38f.

requirement: 'but they did not listen' (7.24, 11.8). In the immediate context of Jeremiah 7 and 11, the answer to this is God's punishment for this sinful Israel. In both chapters the prophet is explicitly forbidden to intercede for 'this people' (7.16, 11.14), because 'this is the people that does not listen to the voice of Yhwh its God' (7.28). Does this mean that the promise God pronounced in the covenant formula, that he will be Israel's God and Israel will be his people, is now revoked and invalid?

We do not know what the 'historical' Jeremiah thought when he spoke these or similar words. Nor do I believe that we should set ourselves to 'reconstruct' this, and in so doing ignore the context of the book of Jeremiah. For this book, in which the message of the prophet Jeremiah has been transmitted to us, rather makes us read on. The next time we encounter the covenant formula is in Jeremiah 24, in the context of the parable about the two baskets of figs. Talking about the good figs, the passage says: 'I will set my eyes upon them for good, and I will bring them back to this land. I will build them up, and not tear them down; I will plant them, and not pluck them up. I will give them a heart to know that I am Yhwh; and they shall be my people and I will be their God, for they shall return to me with their whole heart' (vv. 6f.). This provides an answer to the question just asked. The promise that Israel will be God's people and that he will be Israel's God is not abrogated. Israel's history with God does not end with the accusation that Israel has not listened to God's voice. Instead, with the catastrophe of defeat by the Babylonians and exile for some of the people, a new chapter in this history begins. God gives part of Israel up for lost. But for the other part there is a new beginning.

The most remarkable thing about this announcement of a new beginning is the way in which it links up with what was said earlier. In the call vision, God commissioned Jermiah 'to pluck up and to tear down, to destroy and to overthrow, to build and to plant' (Jer. 1.10). There both the negative-destructive and the positive-constructive aspects of God's acts (which the prophet was to proclaim) are named one after another in the same series. Now they are contrasted—build up, not tear down; plant, not pluck up.[23] The time of God's destructive, annihilating activity will be ended for Israel when the people who are now in exile return to their country again. The declaration of recognition then follows. Here it is linked with the self-introductory formula in its 'pure' form—'that I am Yhwh'—additionally strengthened even more by the preceding 'me' ('to know me').[24] It is therefore a matter of knowing God himself. For this, God will give those he has brought back from exile a heart capable of this knowledge. That is to say, God himself will create the necessary presuppositions, so that the relationship

---

[23] Cf. here R. Bach, 'Bauen und Pflanzen', in *Studien zur Theologie der alttestamentlichen Überlieferungen: Festschrift G. von Rad* (1961), 7–32.

[24] See Chapter III, n. 11.

between God and Israel, which is expressed in the covenant formula that follows, may (again) become reality. For this it is necessary that Israel for its part returns to God. But this is expressed not as a demand but as a fact, as it were: 'for they shall return to me with their whole heart.'

The heart also plays a decisive role in the saying about the 'new covenant', Jer. 31.31–34. This is again an astonishingly dense text, in which a wealth of established theological traditions are united and interwoven. The covenant formula is at the centre of this text. The theological framework is extended, however, by the initial announcement that God will make 'a new covenant' (v. 31). This formulation is unique in the Hebrew Bible. At the same time, to establish this is by no means to imply that the fact expressed in the phrase is new. On the contrary, that a 'new' covenant has taken the place of the original covenant which Israel broke is one of the fundamental elements in the Hebrew Bible's 'covenant theology'. Exodus 32–34 describes quite unambiguously and forcefully how Israel forthwith broke the covenant made with God (24.3–8), by sinning with the Golden Calf. Afterwards there is explicit talk about a renewal of the covenant, even if the word 'new' is not used. The idea of 'a new covenant' is thus implicit in the whole of the Bible's covenant theology from early on: Israel is no longer living in the covenant originally concluded before God and with him, but now lives in the covenant which God has renewed, in spite of Israel's breach of the covenant.[25] The idea in Jeremiah 31 is here already given anticipatory form.

Texts such as Leviticus 26 point in the same direction. Here the subject is first the consequences that will ensue if Israel breaks the b^erît (v. 15), but then in v. 44 the text sets against this God's declaration that he will never break the covenant. Just because of that, he himself 'remembers' the covenant even though the Israelites have broken it (vv. 44f.). In Ezekiel 16 the sweeping presentation of Jerusalem's history in the metaphor of the harlot closes with the divine saying in vv. 59–69. Here the two declarations initially stand directly over against one another: you have broken the covenant—I remember my covenant (vv. 59f.). In this case the covenant which God remembers is more precisely defined as the covenant which God made with Jerusalem 'in the days of her youth'. God will now 'establish' this covenant as 'an everlasting covenant', in spite of Israel's faithlessness (v. 60b).[26] In differing terminology, these texts are putting into words the conviction that the covenant which God has made with Israel will not be broken on God's side, in spite of Israel's sin, but that instead it will be given a new foundation.

---

[25] Cf. Rendtorff, 'Covenant as a Structuring Concept in Genesis and Exodus', in *Canon and Theology* (ET 1993), especially 129ff.; also Dohmen, 'Der Sinaibund als Neuer Bund'.

[26] For this continuity of the covenant, cf. M. Greenberg, *Ezekiel 1–20* (1983), 303.

This is the point at which the image of Israel's heart is brought into play in Jeremiah 31. Jeremiah uses this image rather differently here from the way he employs it in chapter 24. Now the text no longer says that God will give the Israelites a heart 'to know him'; the declaration is now that he 'will put the Torah in their innermost parts and write it into [or: on] their hearts' (v. 33). In both formulations, the point is that God himself will make the hearts of the Israelites capable of knowing him. As in chapter 24, the covenant formula then immediately follows, in 31.33. And again, the knowing of God is directly linked with the covenant formula, this time in a lengthy sentence which says that people will no longer have to teach each other knowledge of God, but 'they will all know me, from the least of them to the greatest' (v. 34).

The special feature of the texts in Jeremiah (and in the book of Ezekiel too) is that the change announced, which is to bring about the renewal of the relationship between God and Israel, will not come about on God's side, but on Israel's. Of course the presupposition here, as in all comparable texts, is that God stands unswervingly by his covenant. But here something is added: God is going to change the presuppositions on Israel's side for the keeping of the covenant. He will put the Torah into Israel's 'innermost parts' and will write it into Israel's heart. So this is really not a new covenant at all; it is the same, unaltered covenant which the forefathers broke (v. 32). What is new are the presuppositions for its acceptance and realisation. Here the text talks about the Torah as the real substance of the covenant—almost in passing, because for this author that was evidently a matter of course. When the Israelites have the Torah in their hearts, God will really be their God, and they will be his people. Here the covenant formula stands at the apex of this concentrated theological programme. The covenant, which always existed, is put into force afresh; and the same is true of Israel's relationship to God. Jeremiah certainly did not formulate the covenant formula here *ad hoc*. He knew it as the expression of the fundamental relationship between God and Israel. What he wants to express with the covenant formula in this connection is on the same level as the declarations about the 'new' covenant. The relationship between God and Israel characterised by the covenant formula also needs renewal: it does not have to be newly created, but it does have to be put into force afresh. Indeed the two things are really identical here—the covenant, and God's relationship to Israel and Israel's to God, which is characterised by the covenant formula. The statement in v. 33 sounds as though the one followed on the other: the new constitution of the relationship to God arises out of a new ability to keep the covenant—and here that means the Torah.

And finally, the whole leads over into a variation of the 'declaration of recognition' (v. 34). This is not simply, as it usually is, 'they will know that I am Yhwh': here a vivid picture describes how there will no

longer be any need to teach the knowledge of God; it will become a
matter of course 'from the least to the greatest'. This brings out the point
that this is not just a matter of 'inwardness': the whole life of individual
and community will be drawn in. But even then this text is not finished.
The final sentence runs: 'for I will forgive their iniquity and will
remember their sin no more'. Here it once again becomes quite clear
that for God to forgive Israel's past sins is the presupposition for this
'new covenant'—and above all that God does not make his adherence
to the covenant and his renewal of it dependent on Israel's conduct.
Here the use of the verb 'remember' is particularly important. Again and
again the Hebrew Bible declares that God remembers his covenant, and
again and again this becomes an essential turning point in the way God
behaves towards Israel. Here, in contrast to this, we now read that God
will not remember Israel's sins.[27] The covenant which God is going to
put into force once more stands in fundamental antithesis to Israel's
sins. In the long run it can and will endure only if God remembers his
covenant but does not remember Israel's sins. And it is just that which
God promises here.

In Jer. 32.36ff. the same theme is sounded as in chapter 24: God will
gather from every country those who have been scattered, will bring
them back to Jerusalem, and will let them dwell there in safety. This
time the covenant formula follows immediately on the announcement of
the 'repatriation' (vv. 37f.). This is reminiscent of the texts in which
the deliverance from Egypt leads immediately into the covenant
formula.[28] So too, therefore, God's bringing back of the exiles to
Jerusalem will be the immediate presupposition that will make it
possible for the relationship between God and Israel to be restored to the
form expressed in the covenant formula. And then we hear again about
the heart which God is going to give Israel (v. 39). Once again the
emphasis is different: God will give them *one* heart, a heart single and
undivided. This is both expanded and more precisely defined through
the phrase 'and *one* way'. The undivided heart is to take the one, straight
path which leads to the fear of God. Again there is a new stress: the fear
of God is moved into the foreground.[29] It is another side of all that is
comprehended in 'the covenant' which God is now going to make anew
with Israel (v. 40). The substance of this newly concluded covenant, or
its consequence, will be that God puts the fear of God into the hearts of
the Israelites. This is again a way of paraphrasing a mutual relationship:
God will not turn away from them, and they will not stray from him.

This covenant is called 'an everlasting covenant'. This places it in a

---

[27] We undoubtedly also find the contrary assertion, that God remembers Israel's sins. In
Jer. 14.10 we have the precise opposite to 31.34. But this very fact shows the progress
towards 'salvation history' within the book of Jeremiah.

[28] See Chapter II.3 above.

[29] The formulations are reminiscent of Deuteronomy, e.g. 4.10, 5.26 and passim.

broad context which begins with God's covenant with Noah and with the whole of creation (Gen. 9.16), and reaches out, by way of the covenant with Abraham (Gen. 17.17 and passim), to the prophets' expectations of the future.[30]

The other two instances of the covenant formula in the book of Jeremiah (Jer. 30.22, 31.1) are not bound into a differentiated, more narrowly defined theological context in the same way as those we have discussed up to now. The function which they have in each case for the overall cohesion of the text in which they now stand would require a precise exegetical investigation which would take us beyond the bounds of this study. But the reader may look at the brief reflections in Chapter II.5b.

In contrast to the book of Jeremiah, in the book of Ezekiel the covenant formula can be encountered solely in salvation oracles pointing towards the future.[31] At the same time, there is again a resemblance to the utterances made in Jeremiah 24 even before the Jerusalem catastrophe, inasmuch as in Ezek. 11.14ff. a saying is addressed to the exiles to whom—unlike those who have stayed behind in 'the land'—God promises a favourable future. He will gather them from their dispersion 'and I will give them the land of Israel' (v. 17). This formulation is significant because it makes the return from exile directly parallel to the gift of the land conferred on the Exodus generation. Here, therefore, the temporal stages of past and future are not distinguished from each other in a strictly logical sense, nor is it said that God will give the exiles the land 'again' or 'afresh'. In this respect there is a clear parallel here to the sayings which speak of a covenant to be made in the impending future, without explicitly either relating this to the previous covenant or calling it new.

The people who return to the land will free it from idolatry (v. 18). Then God will give them a single heart and a new spirit (v. 19). Here again, as in Jer. 32.39, there is talk about an undivided heart. This is not far removed in meaning from a 'new' heart, as the immediately following formulation 'and a new spirit' shows.[32] Ezekiel elaborates this image even more by calling the 'old' heart 'a heart of stone', which God will remove, replacing it by 'a heart of flesh'. Then the text again talks about 'the way' or 'walking'; for the consequence of this change of heart will be that the people will walk the way of God's commandments and will keep his statutes (v. 20). This leads directly into the covenant formula. A comparison with the Jeremiah texts which speak of a different, 'new' heart shows here very clearly that the individual

---

[30] See the present chapter, Section 4.

[31] On Ezekiel 14, see below.

[32] There is no reason to alter the text because of this; cf. Greenberg, *Ezekiel 1–20*, 190. He also draws attention there to a fine parallel in Ps. 86.11: יחד לבבי, 'make my heart undivided'; the continuation ליראה שמך, 'in order to fear your name', is reminiscent of Jer. 32.39.

elements of theological tradition could be woven together in various ways. For example, whereas in Jer. 32.38 the covenant formula provides the starting point for the description of Israel's future conduct (in which the heart then also plays an important part), here in Ezek. 11.20 the formula stands as something like a concluding summary.

The same may be said about the great passage Ezek. 36.22ff. After the catastrophe has fallen on Jerusalem—which 33.21 explicitly names as the decisive datum in the turn of events—God will bring the Israelites back to their land, and will cleanse them from all impurity, for the sake of his holy name, which they have profaned through their sins (vv. 22–25). A passage then follows which is for the most part parallel to 11.19f.: God will give them a new heart and a new spirit; he will take away their heart of stone and plant in them a heart of flesh instead (v. 26). But here the prophetic word goes one step further: 'I will put my spirit in your innermost parts, and make you walk in my commandments and be careful to keep my ordinances and perform them' (v. 27). It is as if God wanted to be quite sure that his commandments are going to be kept. That is why he additionally puts his own spirit into the new heart. And finally, here—as already in Jer. 32.37, and as an important aspect—the promise adds the dwelling in the land, the land which God gave to the forefathers. The covenant formula then follows, again as a summary conclusion (v. 28). It also marks the turning point—the turning to the time that will follow afterwards. God will restore the fertility of the land, thereby making the homecomers ashamed of their sinful behaviour (vv. 29–32). It is here especially that the great importance of the covenant formula is brought out. It gathers together and concludes what was developed in detail beforehand. At the same time it forms the bridge to a new epoch which will dawn when God's promises for the restoration of Israel's relationship to him are fulfilled.

Pollution through the worship of 'idols' is the theme of the passage Ezek. 14.1–11 as well. This is the only one of the sayings including the covenant formula which does not have directly behind it an anticipation of the time after the catastrophe and the return to the land. But when in 'an hour of instruction' the exiles discuss the theme of purification from idolatry, the dominant aspect is still the situation after their hoped-for return. In a long discussion about the questions put to the prophet by an idolater, we are finally told that through the fate of the idolater himself, as well as the fate of the prophet (provided that he has permitted the discussion), the Israelites will be induced to stop defiling themselves in this way. 'And then they shall be my people, and I will be their God' (v. 11). The theme here is much more tightly restricted than it is in other Ezekiel texts. But here again it emerges that the covenant formula is, as it were, the final seal on the restoration of the original relationship between God and Israel, the relationship which God himself desired and initiated.

The obliteration of the defilement by idolatry is also one of the aspects of the vision of the future in Ezek. 37.15–28, a survey envisaging the reunification of Israel and Judah, which will make them once more one people and one kingdom. In v. 23, the covenant formula is directly linked with the announcement of this purification, again as a concluding endorsement of Israel's restored relationship to God. At the same time the covenant formula opens up a further aspect here which was already hinted at in v. 22: the promise of a new David as king over the united kingdom (vv. 24ff.). This is the new situation under the David who has now returned which will lead the people to keep the divine commandments and statutes (v. 24b). Under him they and their descendants will live for ever in this land (v. 25). This assurance reaches its climax in God's promise that he will make a (new) covenant with them, 'a covenant of peace', 'an everlasting covenant'. Neither term is explained in detail here. In Ezek. 34.25 the phrase 'covenant of peace' is related to the protection against wild animals which will make it possible to live safely in the land once more. This echoes Jer. 32.37, where the promise that the people will live safely in the land is also directly linked with the covenant formula. The phrase 'everlasting covenant', on the other hand, points to a wider, overall biblical context, as it already did in Jer. 32.40.[33] Here in Ezekiel 37 there is also an echo of the relation to the divine word given to Abraham in Gen. 17.6, where—as in v. 26b—the 'everlasting covenant' is directly associated with the multiplying of Israel.

Yet another aspect is added at this point: God's dwelling in the midst of Israel (vv. 26b, 27). On the one hand this corresponds to the previous promise that the Israelites will live in safety. God and Israel will live together in the land in which God has set up his sanctuary. On the other hand, there is an echo here of Ex. 29.45. As in the Exodus passage, so here in Ezekiel 37 too the announcement that God will dwell among the Israelites is directly linked with the covenant formula. And in both cases the declaration of recognition follows, although with one great difference: in Exodus 29 the Israelites are to know because of God's dwelling among them that Yhwh is their God, the God who brought them out of Egypt (v. 4); whereas in Ezekiel 37 it is 'the peoples' who are to know that Yhwh is God, the God who sanctifies Israel by setting up his sanctuary among them (v. 28). This is in line with the whole trend of the sayings from Ezek. 36.16 onwards, in which God proclaims that he will save Israel and bring it back, so as to sanctify his holy name again, which Israel has defiled in the sight of the peoples. For that reason the peoples are now the most important witnesses of his being God and of his power. Apart from that we again see here an important parallelism between the 'bringing out' from Egypt and the 'bringing back' from exile.

---

[33] See p. 73 above.

Finally, we encounter the covenant formula yet once more in connection with the announcement of a David *redivivus* in Ezek. 34.23f. The
verses belong to the wider context of a saying directed against 'Israel's
shepherds', in the place of whom God himself will pasture his flock. But
then the text also says that 'my servant David' will pasture the flock. Here
the covenant formula appears, and—for the only time in the book of
Ezekiel—with only one of its elements, the declaration about Yhwh's
being God for Israel (Formula A). It almost seems as if the second
element, which elsewhere talks about Israel's being a people for Yhwh, is
supposed to be replaced by the formulation in v. 24aβ: 'My servant
David prince in their midst'. At the same time the parallel is not completely carried through, since in this sentence the verb היה, 'be', which is
otherwise always used in both halves of the covenant formula, is
missing. However, the fact remains that this is the only time when the covenant
formula is varied in this way. For the coming expectation of a new David
which finds expression here, this can scarcely be overestimated.

In post-exilic prophecy the covenant formula can be found only once
more, in Zech. 8.8. In the collection of sayings in vv. 1–8, which is
divided up by repeated introductory formulas, vv. 7f. have an introduction of their own, in the form of a saying of Yhwh Sabaoth. But at the
same time these verses constitute the conclusion of this little collection,
which in passionate words promises the restoration of Jerusalem (v. 2).
As has already been the case in other contexts of the covenant formula,
God's dwelling in Jerusalem is announced (v. 3), and in the following
vivid descriptions this is brought together with the dwelling of men and
women in Jerusalem (vv. 4f.). There is some doubt whether this
announcement to 'the remnant of the people'—i.e. the homecomers and
those living in Jerusalem now—may not be thought 'too wonderful' (v.
6); but this is countered by the broadly laid-out proclamation of the
liberation of the Israelites who are still scattered among the countries of
the world, a proclamation which closes with the covenant formula (vv.
7f.). As already in other prophetic texts, the covenant formula is, as it
were, the seal on the divine promises for Israel's future, in which the
people will be restored and reinstated in their original relationship to
God. This is emphatically underlined by the concluding phrase, 'in
faithfulness [or: sincerity] and righteousness'. Thus this post-exilic
reverberation of the covenant formula shows that it was still present to
the minds of the people for whom the prophetic promises were already
beginning to be realised, to however modest a degree.

4. *The One, Continually 'New' Covenant*

This is not a study of the 'covenant' as a whole. But in the framework of
our treatment of the covenant formula, we have frequently come up

against questions which are continually asked, and have to be asked, about the covenant too. Consequently in the following section I should like to try to make a contribution from the perspective of the covenant formula to the comprehensive theme of the relationship between God and Israel, which links 'covenant' and 'covenant formula' together. In particular areas, the theme of 'election' will also be included in our considerations. And here one of the most important observations is that the same, or comparable, statements about the relationship between God and Israel as it is expressed in the covenant formula can be made with reference to entirely different epochs in Israel's history. This prompts the question: when was the relationship between God and Israel which was pronounced in the covenant formula constituted, and with whom? Was it constituted once, or several times? How are the declarations about the constitution of this relationship in the past related to others which announce its inception in the imminent or more remote future?

It is sufficiently obvious that the same, or similar, questions could be asked with reference to God's covenant with Israel too. Moreover, in many cases covenant formula and covenant are so closely interwoven in the texts that the questions and the possible answers could apply to both. And in each case, furthermore, it is difficult to arrive at answers because the texts themselves offer little information. Where the covenant is concerned, the fact that the word $b^e r\hat{\imath}t$ occurs only in the singular puts an obstacle in the way of talk about different 'covenants'.[34] Things are very similar in the case of the covenant formula. The linguistic formulations are firmly fixed, and allow us to detect very little about different temporal aspects.

Let us begin with the question about these temporal aspects. The linguistic formulations of the covenant formula themselves offer no peg on which to hang a decision as to whether the relationship with God is definitively established, or brought into being, at the moment when the covenant formula is pronounced, or whether this relationship is promised for the future. As we saw in Chapter III.1, the formulations are stereotyped, as it were. Linguistically they always contain a 'final' or purposive element, or one pointing to the future, whether this be in the form of 'in order to be', or whether it be the future perfect consecutive, with or without a following imperfect. In a number of cases, however, the context makes a decision possible. This is true above all when the covenant formula points to something in the past, especially the deliverance from Egypt. As we have seen, this is the case in most of the texts with formula A (about Yhwh's being God) in the Priestly Pentateuch,[35] and is also true of Deut. 4.20, where formula B (about

---

[34] Cf. J. Barr, 'Some Semantic Notes on the Covenant', in *Beiträge zur alttestamentlichen Theologie: Festschrift W. Zimmerli* (1977), 29: '$b^e r\hat{\imath}t$ forms no plural; it is strange that this fact is not more frequently commented upon'.

[35] Lev. 11.45, 22.32f., 25.38, 26.45; Num. 15.41.

Israel's being a people) is used. In these instances the formula says unequivocally that God established his relationship to Israel in the past through the deliverance from Egypt.

But did this relationship between God and Israel not already exist before that? Here the question about the covenant enters the arena. In Gen. 17.7 the text reads: 'I will establish (וַהֲקִמֹתִי) my covenant with you'—and then covenant formula A follows, introduced by לִהְיוֹת, 'in order to be'. Here the covenant formula is an exposition of the covenant's content: the two are identical, so to speak. Does this now mean that God is setting up the covenant at this particular moment? Or does the formula point to the future? The rest of the text in Genesis 17 speaks clearly in favour of the former; for in vv. 9ff. Abraham is exhorted to keep the covenant, which accordingly must already exist. The findings in Exodus 6 are less ambiguous still, for v. 4 reads: 'I established my covenant with them' (i.e. the patriarchs), and v. 5b: 'therefore I remember my covenant'. The covenant made in the past exists, and is the foundation for God's behaviour to Israel which is now announced. Yet here too the covenant formula contains the 'future' element by way of the two verbal forms in the perfect consecutive: 'I will take you to be my people and will be God for you' (v. 7). In the first instance it would seem obvious that God is going to take Israel for his people only in the immediate future, especially since the recognition formula which follows speaks of the deliverance from Egypt which is still to come. But a future interpretation in the narrower sense seems hardly plausible for the second declaration about God's being God, since Yhwh's being God for Israel was, after all, already constituted through the covenant made with Abraham. Here, in my view, the fixed, formula-like character of the pronouncement must be taken into account. Its content is repeated and thereby substantially confirmed. God will continue to be Israel's God, from now on under altered presuppositions.

The same may be said about Ex. 29.45. God announces that after the sanctuary has been built he will live there, among the Israelites, 'and I will be God for them'. The new thing here is the announcement that God is going to live in the midst of Israel. This again creates new presuppositions for God's relationship to Israel, and his being God for Israel is hence emphatically confirmed. The recognition formula which follows (v. 26) underlines this interpretation: God has brought Israel out of Egypt, and according to many declarations in the Pentateuch has in so doing constituted his relationship to Israel.[36] But the newly added aspect is that one important reason for the deliverance was that God now wishes to live in the midst of the Israelites. The same formulation can also be found in Lev. 26.12. There the beginning of the great final chapter on the law-giving on Sinai describes what will happen if Israel

[36] See n. 35.

keeps God's commandments (vv. 3ff.). God will give abundant blessing and will finally 'establish' (וַהֲקִימֹתִי) his covenant. Here we
are faced with the same question about the relation between the
constituting of the covenant that belongs to the past, and the statement
in the text, which points to the future. But the question is somewhat
different here, since the verb הקים can be used to designate both the act
of 'establishing' the covenant and its 'observance'.[37] Then God will
dwell in the midst of Israel—and the covenant formula in its two-term
form (C) follows (v. 12). Here too what is being spoken of is evidently
not a new constitution of the covenant relationship, but its endorsement
and realisation.

This being so, for the Priestly Pentateuch there can be no doubt that
God made the covenant with which he constituted the mutual relationship between himself and Israel with Abraham first of all, or with the
'forefathers', i.e. the patriarchs. But at the same time it is clear that this
relationship is continually called to remembrance and confirmed whenever new presuppositions or constellations arise. This fact can occasionally give rise to what seems at first sight to be a contradictory 'doublet'.
In Lev. 26.42ff., for example, God first remembers his covenant with the
patriarchs Jacob, Isaac and Abraham by turning once more to the
Israelites who are exiled from 'the land' (v. 42). But the text goes on to
say that he remembers the covenant with 'those of former times' whom
he brought out of Egypt (v. 45). It is quite obvious that this does not
mean that there were two different covenants. Rather, the covenant with
the patriarchs, who also received the promise of the land, was given
concrete form (and in this respect its fulfilment) when Israel was
brought out of Egypt, the aim of that deliverance being to bring Israel
into the land promised to the patriarchs.

The interweaving of the deliverance from Egypt with God's covenant with the patriarchs is very close in other passages too. The
fundamental passage for this is first of all again Exodus 6, where the
announcement of the deliverance from Egypt is called a 'remembering'—i.e. a fulfilment of the covenant made with the patriarchs (v. 4f.).
The wording with which Deut. 7.8 follows the covenant formula and
the declaration of election in v. 6 is very similar: 'Because Yhwh ...
has kept the oath that he swore to your forefathers, Yhwh has brought
you out with a mighty hand'. This is substantially reminiscent of
Exodus 6, even if a different terminology is used when the text talks
about God's 'oath' to the forefathers. In Deut. 29.11f. <12f.> God's
oath to the patriarchs is cited with the bilateral covenant formula as the
immediate justification or foundation for the establishment of the
relationship with God, although here the deliverance from Egypt is not

---

[37] Cf. W. Schottroff, *'Gedenken' im Alten Orient und im Alten Testament* (2nd edn.,
1967), 208; J. Gamberoni, 'קוּם *qûm*', ThWAT 6 (1989), 1263.

mentioned. The intermediate generation is skipped over, so to speak. In Jer. 11.3–5 the 'forefathers' appear twice: God charged the forefathers to obey 'the words of his covenant' when he brought them out of Egypt (vv. 3f.). But he delivered them in order to 'establish' (i.e. to put into force) the oath which he swore to the forefathers that he would give them the land (v. 5). The members of two different generations are therefore termed 'forefathers' here: the patriarchs, to whom God gave the promise of the land, and the Exodus generation, for whom the promise was implemented.[38] This shows once more that we must be cautious here about imposing 'logical' demands on the texts. For Israel, the traditions about God's covenant with the forefathers are associated with different stages of its history, and the one cannot be played off against the other.[39] The same may also be said about Jer. 31.32, which says that God made a covenant with the forefathers when he brought them out of Egypt. According to the context, what is meant here is the aspect which Jer. 11.3f. terms 'the words of this covenant which I commanded your forefathers when I brought them out of the land of Egypt'. The earliest generation of forefathers is not mentioned at this point, nor is any such mention required in view of the theme of this section of text. But it would be bizarre to conclude from this that the author of this text knew nothing about God's covenant with Abraham and the other patriarchs.

The question about the temporal aspects of the making of the covenant comes to a head in the formulations in Deuteronomy in particular. According to what is said there, the relation between God and Israel is essentially constituted 'today': 'Hear O Israel, today you have become a people for Yhwh your God' (Deut. 27.9). Associated with this is the command to listen to God's voice and to fulfil his precepts and commandments (v. 10). In 5.1–4 this 'today' stands in stressed antithesis to the generations of the 'forefathers': 'Not with our fore-fathers did Yhwh make this covenant but with us, who are all of us here alive today' (v. 3). If we are to understand this apparent antithesis we must take in the previous sentence: 'Yhwh our God made a covenant with us at Horeb' (v. 2). So this is not a matter of an antithesis between the former generation and the generation of today: this is an identifica-tion of the two. Today's generation *is* the Horeb generation. The covenant was made, not with an earlier generation but with the present one. The concern is clear: the covenant given at Horeb is not a thing of the past. It belongs to the present. The words 'not with our forefathers' are in no way meant to disparage the earlier generation, as if it had no

[38] See the debate between Römer and Lohfink referred to in n. 22, especially Lohfink, *Die Väter Israels*, 38f.

[39] Barr's remark, 'distinctions where no distinction is meant' ('Some Semantic Notes on the Covenant', 37), does not apply only to Kutsch (see n. 43 below).

share in the covenant. What they wish to do, however, is to set the present generation in the decisive situation of people with whom God is making the covenant here and now. The paranetic intention is patent.[40] Consequently these texts provide no answer to the question whether Israel was already 'a people for Yhwh'—or stood in a covenant relationship to God—before this 'today'. But in the framework of Deuteronomy as a whole the question can be unequivocally answered: both God's commitment to the Exodus generation and the retrospective link with the patriarchs are articulated often enough, and with sufficient clarity. Consequently this emphatic concentration on the present situation cannot be viewed as a departure from the tradition according to which God had already entered into a covenant relationship with the patriarchs, and then with the Exodus generation.

But this again raises the question whether the 'covenants' which God made with the different generations were different covenants. Let us first consider the question from the perspective of the covenant formula, since this is the actual subject of our present study. Here the answer is that—in spite of some variants—there are no differences in the formulations of the covenant formula, whether these relate to the patriarchs, to the deliverance from Egypt, to the encounter with God at Sinai/Horeb, or to a 'new' covenant still impending.[41] Nor does the formula ever include any indication as to whether a relationship with God in the sense of the covenant formula already existed; nor is the question ever asked whether God wishes to revoke or end the relationship to Israel once it has been constituted.[42] In the canonical context of the Hebrew Bible, therefore, it must be said that God laid the foundation for his relationship to Israel in his covenant with Abraham (Genesis 17) and then, with the Exodus generation, extended it to the people of Israel (Exodus 6). In both cases, covenant formula and the word $b^e r \hat{\imath} t$ are closely interwoven, the covenant formula here interpreting the word $b^e r \hat{\imath} t$, as it were.

From this point of departure, there can in fact really be no other, further covenant. The covenant has been made once and for all, and at its very foundation God had already called it an 'everlasting covenant' (Gen. 17.7, 19). At the same time, emphases in the way the covenant is

---

[40] Lohfink, *Die Väter Israels*, 23f.

[41] Even the special case of the Jehoiada covenant in II Kings 11.17 does not deviate in its formulation.

[42] Here the question arises whether Hos. 1.9 belongs to this context. This is an interesting question in several respects, not least because all the other texts with the covenant formula are Deuteronomic or later. But in Hosea too the restoration of the covenant relationship denied in 1.9 is pronounced in 2.25 <23>. Cf. the discussions in R. Smend, 'Die Bundesformel', in *Die Mitte des Alten Testaments: Gesammelte Studien* 1 (1986), 31ff., and in Lohfink, 'Dt 26, 17–19 und die "Bundesformel"', in *Studien zum Deut.* 1 (1990), 260f., as well as in the commentaries on Hosea.

spoken of do shift, and so do the facets of its content which become the
focus of attention. In the texts which speak of the covenant with the
patriarchs and the deliverance from Egypt, God's promise and his
helping and saving acts are dominant. In other texts, beginning above all
with Israel's encounter with God at Sinai, the obligation which God laid
on the Israelites, and the observance of which he requires, comes to the
fore. Nevertheless, a closer examination shows that there is no antithesis
between these two aspects. On this point, it is important to note first that
at the very foundation of the covenant in Genesis 17, it is not only God's
promise to Abraham that is a constituent element of the covenant; this is
equally true of Abraham's obligation: 'You shall keep my covenant, you
and your descendants after you throughout their generations' (v. 9).
Here it is the circumcision which has to be observed, as forerunner and
as 'earnest' or pledge, so to speak, of the full Torah, thus being a 'sign
of the covenant' (v. 11), and itself also being termed an 'everlasting
covenant'.[43] In this respect it is not surprising when at the arrival at Sinai
the proclamation of the first commandment is prefaced by: 'If you listen
to my voice and keep my covenant' (Ex. 19.5). Israel knows (or, to be
more precise, the reader knows) that the covenant has to be 'kept'. It is
the same formulation as in Genesis 17.[44]

This second aspect comes more prominently to the fore as the
Pentateuch goes on, however, so that occasionally one might get the
impression that it is a different kind of relationship to God which is
under discussion here. This impression is most tersely and unambiguously given in Deut. 27.9f.: 'Hear O Israel, today you have become a
people for Yhwh your God; and you shall listen to the voice of Yhwh
your God and act according to the precepts and commandments that I
am commanding you today'. Here there is no pointer to other aspects of
what being a people for Yhwh means. But this is evidently due to the
immediate context. In the ceremonial 'conclusion of the covenant' in
Deut. 26.16–19, the fulfilment of the commandments is certainly also
central; but in the term 'people for his possession' (v. 18) there is
already a hint of election terminology and in v. 19 this is then explicated
still further with the idea that Israel has been raised up above all peoples,
and through the expression 'holy people'. Thus the understanding of the
relationship between God and Israel which underlies this passage is
clearly related to texts such as Deut. 7.6 and 14.2, where the idea of
election is dominant.

Various texts talk about a correlation between the keeping of the

---

[43] E. Kutsch, *Verheißung und Gesetz* (1973), 142, demonstrates that the carefully
crafted structure of Genesis 17 (on which see Chapter II, n. 22 above) has to be destroyed
if one wishes to maintain an antithesis here between two different covenants. On Genesis
17 cf. also F. Crüsemann, *The Torah* (ET 1996), 294f.

[44] Dohmen also draws attention to the connection between Exodus 19 and Genesis 17;
see 'Der Sinaibund als Neuer Bund', 76.

commandments and what God does; and this was already suggested in Ex. 19.6. Thus Lev. 26.3–13—introducing what it says by 'if you walk in my commandments'—describes the consequences of observing the divine commandments, which will be abundant blessing and peace, an outcome which reaches its climax in the establishing of the covenant and in the confirmation of God's relationship to Israel. The continuation in vv. 14ff. poses the contrast. It begins with the words 'But if you do not listen to me' and describes in highly comprehensive and dramatic terms the negative consequences of disobedience, which will be catastrophes of every kind. Here we get the impression that the continuance of the relationship to God endorsed by the covenant depends on Israel's fulfilment of the commandments. But at the end of the chapter this impression is explicitly rejected as false: God does not break his covenant; on the contrary, he remembers it, and renews his promise to be God for Israel (vv. 42–45).[45]

How does this relate to the formulation in Exodus 19? When the passage says '*If* you listen to my voice and keep my covenant, [then] you shall be my possession out of all peoples', are these words meant as a condition? What would happen if Israel did not listen to God's voice, or did not listen to it any more, and did not keep the covenant? Here it is important to notice first of all that in Ex. 19.5 the covenant itself is not up for discussion. It exists independently of Israel's behaviour; but Israel can and should keep it. If Israel does so, it should and will be God's 'possession'. The result of Israel's conduct therefore does not affect the covenant; what it does affect is Israel's special position in relation to God.[46] In the context of the Pentateuch, two things then emerge: Israel does not listen to God's voice, but turns to other gods in the form of the Golden Calf (Ex. 32.1–6). But God stands by his covenant and renews it (34.10). This is at the same time an answer to Moses's plea that God should forgive Israel's sins (v. 9). In this respect one might even go so far as to say that the covenant announced in 34.10 is a 'new' covenant. Seen from God's side, it is the same covenant which he had already made with Abraham and confirmed for the Exodus generation. But in turning aside from the way which God had marked out for it with the covenant, Israel has now called the premise in question from its side. God now of his own accord creates this premise anew by forgiving Israel's sin and confirming the covenant afresh, in

---

[45] Deuteronomy 28 is in many respects comparable with Leviticus 26. But here the renewal of the covenant and the relationship to God follows only in the succeeding chapters, Deuteronomy 29–32.

[46] This distinction has been especially stressed by Dohmen, 'Der Sinaibund als Neuer Bund', 71f. His observations are also the basis of the following reflections, which I had already expressed in brief form in 1989 in '"Covenant" as a Structuring Concept', 129ff.

full awareness that Israel is a 'stiff-necked' people (v. 9).[47,48] Thus the restoration of the covenant relationship in Lev. 26.42–45 is along exactly the same lines.

From this point we turn almost of necessity to Jer. 31.31–34, which speaks explicitly of the 'new covenant'. The reader who comes from Exodus 32–34 and Leviticus 26 is not surprised by the judgement that the forefathers of the Exodus generation broke the covenant (v. 32). The announcement that God is going to react to this by confirming the covenant afresh (v. 31b) is not new to the reader either. Ex. 34.10 has already used the verb כרת ('make'; literally 'cut') for this, a word which does not merely designate the first institution of the covenant relationship, but its renewed enactment as well. It is the latter which is meant in Jeremiah 31 too, the renewed and re-enacted covenant here being expressly termed 'new' for the first (and only) time. But in substance the parallelism with the renewed establishment and endorsement of the covenant in Ex. 34.10 is quite clear. An essential point in this connection is that in both texts the new establishment of the covenant is indissolubly linked with the forgiveness of Israel's sins. In Exodus 34, Moses's plea in v. 9 that Israel's sins be forgiven immediately precedes the restitution of the covenant. In Jeremiah 31 the promise of forgiveness is placed in an emphatic position at the end (v. 34), thereby reinforcing the need for the forgiveness of sins as the basis for the new covenant, and at the same time stressing God's readiness to forgive, in order that this covenant may be maintained.[49]

At the centre of the passage Jer. 31.31–34 we find a sentence which links together two elements: the more specific definition of the substance of the new covenant, and the covenant formula in its two-term form (v. 33aβ-b). The tenor of the new covenant will be that God puts his Torah 'in their innermost parts and writes it on their heart'. This is hinted at in Deut. 30.1–14, where the link between Israel's heart and the fulfilment of the divine commandments is expressed under various aspects. God will bring Israel back from exile, and he will 'circumcise your heart and the heart of your descendants, so that you can love Yhwh your God with all your heart and with all your soul' (v. 6). This will find expression through Israel's listening to Yhwh's voice and observing all his commandments (v. 8; cf. v. 10). And finally the text even says that God's commandment is not far from Israel, not in heaven or beyond the sea: 'No, the word is very near to you, in your mouth and in your heart,

---

[47] This is also E. Aurelius's interpretation in *Der Fürbitter Israels* (1988), 116–126.

[48] Here the parallel with the covenant made with Noah in Genesis 9 is especially significant (cf. Rendtorff, '"Covenant" as a Structuring Concept', 130). I cannot follow up this important relationship here, since it is outside the scope of the covenant formula, which of course only emerges with Abraham's call.

[49] Cf. here Dohmen, 'Der Sinaibund als Neuer Bund', 78. According to Dohmen, 'the forgiveness of sins of Jer. 31.34 is the foundation for all the promises of Jer. 30.1–31.34'.

so that you may fulfil it' (v. 14). This text from Deuteronomy manifests the same train of thought as Jeremiah 31: from the exile as the consequence of the breach of the covenant, to a new beginning, in which the heart will be 'circumcised', so that it can be the vehicle of the divine commandment.

In Jeremiah 31 this progression of ideas now reaches its climax in the covenant formula (v. 33b). Here again we can see the central function which the covenant formula can continually assume. Here it acts as explication of the actual content of the covenant. The sentence which begins with the words 'And this will be the covenant that I will make with the house of Israel' points toward the covenant formula. When the Torah is put into Israel's innermost parts and written on its heart, this is to make enduringly possible the continued existence of the relationship between God and Israel which the covenant formula expresses: 'I will be their God and they shall be my people'. With this, the text moves into direct continuity with those texts in which the covenant formula itself expresses the object of the covenant relationship: Gen. 17.7 and Deut. 29.12 <13>.[50] What began with Abraham and was endorsed at Horeb will once more be reinforced afresh 'in those days', and will be made indestructible through the renewal of Israel's heart.

5. *The Exegetical and Theological Importance of the Covenant Formula*

At the end of our investigation, it may be useful to make a brief résumé, gathering together the most important results in their bearing on the exegetical and theological function of the covenant formula. The investigation has moved deliberately and consistently on the synchronic level of the final text of the Hebrew Bible. But through occasional comments I have tried to make it clear that in some cases I fully recognise the importance of diachronic questions; and I should expressly like to invite readers to follow up these questions further, and not to see this pursuit as irreconcilable with the outline put forward here. One diachronic aspect, indeed, has already emerged from the very layout of the investigation, since on the grounds of the way Deuteronomy deals with the covenant formula, it had to be treated separately from the rest of the Pentateuch. The use of the term 'Priestly Pentateuch' is also a way of making the point that here the subject of our study is the use of the covenant formula in the Priestly stratum of the Pentateuch's composition.

In this Priestly composition we can see the first clear signals of an extremely deliberate and theologically thought-through use of the covenant formula. The key features are marked out by Genesis 17 and

---

[50] See p. 68 above.

Exodus 6. In both cases the covenant formula is very closely linked with the term *b^erît*, 'covenant'; indeed the formula may be positively said to be an exposition of what the word *b^erît* means. God establishes his covenant with Abraham 'in order to be God for you and for your descendants after you' (Gen. 17.7). Yhwh's being God for Abraham is the real substance of this covenant. Later, when Israel cries out to God in its Egyptian slavery, God 'remembers' this covenant which he established with the patriarchs, and extends it to the whole people: 'I will take you for my people and will be God for you' (Ex. 6.4f., 7).

Outside the Priestly Pentateuch too the covenant formula appears as an explication of the covenant. Thus in Deuteronomy 29, at the beginning of Moses's first great speech after the recital of the compendium of commandments, the passage says that God is making the covenant with Israel in solemn form, 'in order this day to raise you up to be a people for him, and he will be God for you' (v. 12 <13>). Here, through the coda 'as he told you and as he swore to your forefathers Abraham, Isaac and Jacob', the text emphatically stresses that this covenant made at Horeb stands in continuity with the covenant made with the patriarchs. At the same time it is clear here that an arc is thus being spanned from Abraham to the Exodus community gathered together at Horeb.

Finally, the 'new covenant' in Jeremiah 31 is also defined through the covenant formula. The essential declaration which announces what the new covenant will consist of leads over to the covenant formula: 'I will be God for them, and they shall be a people for me' (v. 33b). Here too the continuity with the covenant already made earlier with the patriarchs is maintained, even if it takes the form of a radical criticism of the conduct of 'the forefathers'—and for Jeremiah that means all generations since the deliverance from Egypt. And yet the new covenant is going to confirm the previous one inasmuch as its essential content is, and will remain, the mutual relationship between God and Israel.

Thus at essential points the covenant formula is presented as an explication of the substance of God's covenant with Israel. Moreover it is notable that this is the case in all the three great complexes or spheres in which the covenant formula occurs: in the Priestly Pentateuch, in Deuteronomy, and in the prophetic books. In the Pentateuch the structuring function of the covenant formula is clearly detectable, while this is not true for the other complexes to the same extent.

In Jeremiah 31 the covenant formula simultaneously has an essential function in one of the texts which talk about Israel's breach of the covenant, and God's renewal of it. That puts the text into the same context as a number of other passages. In Genesis 17 the covenant is already linked with the obligation to 'keep it', in this case by way of the circumcision (vv. 9ff.). To infringe this obligation is designated a breach of the covenant, and incurs the threat of severe punishment (v. 14). But here that applies only to the individual who is guilty of this offence, not to the community as a whole.[51] Consequently no declaration about the continuance or renewal of the covenant need be expected. Leviticus 26 is a different matter. There, in the great chapter of blessing and curse, the second phase is introduced by the pronouncement that the Israelites are breaking the covenant (vv. 14f.). By so doing they are withdrawing from the relationship to God which was expressed immediately beforehand through the covenant formula. At the end of the chapter this is then set against the announcement that in spite of all Israel's sins God will not break his covenant (v. 44), but will remember it, and restore the relationship to Israel which the covenant formula affirmed (vv. 42, 45). This theme is also treated in a number of important texts in which the covenant formula does not appear. This applies especially to the central text complex in Ex. 32–34 about the breach of the covenant and its reinstallation. It is true that in the reference text Ex. 19.5 a modification of the covenant formula appears in the formulation 'if you keep my covenant'; but in Exodus 34, which speaks of the renewal of the covenant after it has been breached, the covenant formula is missing.[52] It must, however, be said that an explicit mention of the covenant's 'breach' is also missing in these two texts.[53]

A particularly notable point is that when the covenant formula is used, it appears at what might be called the first and last cornerstones stones in the speech about the covenant relationship between God and Israel: in central texts dealing with its establishment at the beginning, and with its ultimate stage, which still lies in the future. Again Genesis 17 and Exodus 6 must be mentioned first here, passages in which God's covenant with Abraham is established and then extended to the whole people. In both cases, covenant formula and covenant are closely linked. In Deuteronomy, the founding of the relationship between God and Israel is characterised particularly by the concept of election. In Deut. 7.6 and 14.2 the word 'choose' (בחר) is directly associated with the covenant formula: 'Yhwh has chosen you to be a people for his own possession out of all peoples'. So the election is an election to be God's people, as the covenant formula says (here in formula B, about Israel's being a people for Yhwh). In a slightly different formulation, Deut. 4.20 says that Israel is to be for God 'the people of his own inheritance'. Here, in accord with Deuteronomy's way of thinking and speaking, the gaze is turned above all to the presence of the Israel gathered together at Horeb, so that the election occasionally seems to coincide with the

---

[51] See W. Thiel, 'Hēfēr berît: Zum Bundbrechen im Alten Testament', VT 20 (1970), 227.

[52] From the diachronic viewpoint, this gives rise to the assumption that the covenant formula represents a theological structural element deliberately introduced by the Priestly redaction—an element which was not introduced in detail into the pre-Priestly texts.

[53] Cf. the chart in Thiel, 'Hēfēr berît', 214.

deliverance from Egypt (especially in 4.20). But it is retrospectively bound to God's oath to the forefathers (especially in 7.6ff.), so that the beginning instituted with the patriarchs is drawn in.

In the prophetic books of Jeremiah and Ezekiel, the centre of gravity of declarations using the covenant formula then shifts to the still impending future of the final, untroubled relationship between God and Israel. This begins with the image of the two baskets of figs in Jeremiah 24, where God announces to the exiles the restoration of the relationship described by the covenant formula, now linked with the gift of a heart able to know him (v. 7). This promise reaches its culmination in the speech about the 'new covenant' in Jer. 31.31–34. In Jer. 32.38–40 the promise is reiterated once more, the future covenant now being called an 'everlasting covenant'. We find a very similar viewpoint in the book of Ezekiel, where the new establishment of Israel's relationship to God in the end-time is proclaimed again and again with the covenant formula (Ezek. 11.20, 36.26–28, 37.21ff.; cf. 34.24). In Ezek. 37.26f. the 'everlasting covenant' is simultaneously promised as 'a covenant of peace'.

A comparison of the texts in which the covenant formula designates either the beginning of the relationship between God and Israel or its eschatological future acquires yet another special aspect with the announcement that God will 'dwell' among the Israelites. One instance is Ex. 29.45 where, at the close of the instructions about the erection of the sanctuary and the institution of daily sacrifice, the text reads: 'I will dwell in the midst of the Israelites, and I will be God for them'. In the recognition formula that follows, God's dwelling in the midst of Israel is once more called the goal of the deliverance from Egypt (v. 46). The same announcement is repeated in Leviticus 26. God will set up his dwelling in the midst of Israel and will walk in its midst—and then the covenant formula follows (vv. 11f.). This is echoed in Ezek. 37.26–28. Here God promises the Judaeans and Israelites, reunited in their land under a new King David, that he will make with them a covenant of peace, an everlasting covenant, and will set up his sanctuary, his dwelling, in their midst—and then the covenant formula follows once more. And the importance of the sanctuary erected in the midst of Israel is stressed once more, since from that the peoples will know 'that I am Yhwh, who sanctifies Israel, because my sanctuary will be in the midst of them for evermore'. The cast back of this promise to the texts in Exodus and Leviticus is patent, especially since the word for the sanctuary, משכן, 'dwelling', never occurs anywhere else in the book of Ezekiel. In Zech. 8.1–8, the announcement that God will dwell in the midst of Jerusalem (v. 3) appears in a somewhat wider context with the covenant formula (v. 8). But the link between the two is clearly forged because v. 8, in direct association with the covenant formula, reads, in a word-for-word parallel to v. 3, 'my people ... shall dwell in the midst of

Jerusalem'.[54] So we again see here the covenant formula in its function of spanning the whole range of God's acts with Israel from the beginning until the end-time goal still to come.

Another important characteristic of the covenant formula is its frequent association with other formula-like elements.[55] Moreover it becomes plain that this link is by no means 'formula-like' in a negative sense, but that it is employed in a process of highly conscious reflection. This may especially be said where the 'recognition formula' is concerned. The starting point in this case too is the passage Ex. 6.2–8. The covenant formula is directly followed up in v. 7b by the recognition formula. Because God takes Israel to be his people and will himself be Israel's God, Israel is to know, first and foremost, 'that I am Yhwh, your God'.[56] Knowledge of Yhwh's identity is then anchored to a succinct survey of God's previous and future history with Israel: the deliverance from Egypt, the bringing into the promised land, the earlier oath to the patriarchs that God would give them the land, and finally the transference of the land to Israel's possession.

The same link between covenant formula and recognition formula can be seen in Ex. 29.45f. Again the declaration of recognition joins directly on to the covenant formula, and again its primary, essential substance is the knowledge 'that I am Yhwh their God'. Here too the further exposition includes first of all the declaration about the deliverance from Egypt; but it then goes on to what is the specific concern of this text: 'in order to dwell in your midst'. In Deut. 7.6–11 the sequence of the individual elements is reversed. First comes the declaration of election, closely interwoven with the covenant formula (v. 6); then follows the recapitulation of God's historical acts with Israel, from the oath to the patriarchs to the deliverance from Egypt; and finally, as conclusion, comes the recognition formula (v. 9). This time too, the first point is the knowing of Yhwh himself, though here in the specifically Deuteronomic form 'that Yhwh your God alone is God'.[57] A list of other attributes of God follows.

In Jer. 24.7 the link between covenant formula and recognition formula is different again. In this case the recognition formula comes at the beginning: God will give Israel a heart to know him. The object of knowledge is here solely 'that I am Yhwh', and then the covenant formula follows. In the complex texture of Jer. 31.31–34, the recognition declaration again comes right at the end, in immediate proximity to the covenant formula, although here it is split up into the announcement that no one will teach anyone else, saying 'know Yhwh!', but they will

---

[54] In Ezekiel 37 the correspondence between the dwelling of the Israelites and the dwelling of God is not quite so unequivocal, since in v. 25 the verb ישׁי is used, not שׁכן.

[55] See Chapter III.4 above.

[56] On the 'self-introductory formula', see below.

[57] Cf. R. Rendtorf, '*'El* als israelitische Gottesbezeichnung', *ZAW* 106 (1994), 19.

all know him. In Ezek. 37.26–28 the recognition formula also follows immediately on the covenant formula, but with the surprising new twist that it is the peoples who will know 'that I am Yhwh', and will know it because he has established his sanctuary in Israel's midst, in that way sanctifying Israel.

It is notable that again the link between covenant formula and recognition formula can be found in all three complexes—Priestly Pentateuch, Deuteronomy and the prophetic books. Another observation is important too: in these texts the recognition formula is often associated with the self-introductory formula, and in such a way that the declaration 'I am Yhwh' is in each case the first element of what is to be known. With the sole exception of Jeremiah 31.31–34, this is the case in all the texts we have just cited (Ex. 6.7, 29.45f.; Jer. 24.7; and Ezek. 37.28, as well as Deut. 7.6 and 7. 9, in slightly varied form). In Ex. 6.2–8 the self-introductory formula additionally plays a role of its own, structuring the whole passage through its triple occurrence in vv. 2, 6 and 8. The formula acts as a similar structural element in Lev. 11.44f., where it is twice used as introductory formula (vv. 44 and 45); here the recognition formula is absent. It is missing in Lev. 26.12f. too, where the self-introductory formula follows directly on the covenant formula.

It therefore emerges under the most diverse aspects that in important sectors of the Hebrew Bible the covenant formula is an element of theological language which is introduced in a highly conscious manner. It expresses in an extremely pregnant way God's relationship to Israel and Israel's to God. At the same time it combines with other terms, above all 'covenant' and 'choose', as well as with other elements of the theological language, such as the recognition formula and the self-introductory formula, each of which has its own significance and function. In many cases it binds these elements together and interprets them afresh, or creates new theological coherences through their association. In this way the covenant formula contributes essentially to the expression and differentiation of the thematic field which may be summarily termed 'covenant theology'.

APPENDIX

Table of Formulas with להיות לי

A	Gen. 17.7b	להיות לך לאלהים
A	Gen. 17.8b	והייתי להם לאלהים
C	**Ex. 6.7**	ולקחתי אתכם לי לעם
C	**Ex. 6.7**	והייתי לכם לאלהים
A	Ex. 29.45	והייתי להם לאלהים
A	Lev. 11.45	להית לכם לאלהים
A	Lev. 22.33	להיות לכם לאלהים
A	Lev. 25.38	להיות לכם לאלהים
C	**Lev. 26.12**	והייתי לכם לאלהים
C	**Lev. 26.12**	ואתם תהיו־לי לעם
A	Lev. 26.45	להיות להם לאלהים
A	Num. 15.41	להיות לכם לאלהים
<u>B</u>	<u>Deut. 4.20</u>	להיות לו לעם נחלה
<u>B</u>	<u>Deut. 7.6</u>	(בחר) להיות לו לעם סגלה מכל העמים
<u>B</u>	<u>Deut. 14.2</u>	(בחר) להיות לו לעם סגלה מכל העמים
C	**Deut. 26.17**	להיות לך לאלהים (וללכת)
C	**Deut. 26.19**	להיות לו לעם סגלה
<u>B</u>	<u>Deut. 27.9</u>	נהיית לעם ליהוה אלהיך
<u>B</u>	<u>Deut. 28.9</u>	יקימך יהוה לו לעם קדוש
C	**Deut. 29.12 <13>**	למען הקים־אתך היום לו לעם
C	**Deut. 29.12 <13>**	והוא יהיה־לך לאלהים
<u>B</u>	<u>I Sam. 12.22</u>	כי הואיל יהוה לעשות אתכם לו לעם
C	**II Sam. 7.24**	ותכונן לך את־עמך ישראל לך לעם עד־עולם
C	**II Sam. 7.24**	ואתה יהוה היית להם לאלהים
<u>B</u>	<u>II Kings 11.17</u>	להיות לעם ליהוה
C	**Jer. 7.23**	והייתי לכם לאלהים ואתם תהיו לי לעם
C	**Jer. 11.4**	והייתם לי לעם ואנכי אהיה לכם לאלהים
<u>B</u>	<u>Jer. 13.11</u>	להיות לי לעם
C	**Jer. 24.7**	והיו־לי לעם ואנכי אהיה להם לאלהים
C	**Jer. 30.22**	והייתם לי לעם ואנכי אהיה לכם לאלהים
C	**Jer. 31.1**	אהיה לאלהים לכל משפחות ישראל והמה יהיו־לי לעם
C	**Jer. 31.33**	והייתי להם לאלהים והמה יהיו לי לעם

93

C	Jer. 32.38	והיו לי לעם ואני אהיה להם לאלהים
C	Ezek. 11.20	והיה־לי לעם ואני אהיה להם לאלהים
C	Ezek. 14.11	והיו־לי לעם ואני אהיה להם לאלהים
A	Ezek. 34.24	ואני יהוה אהיה להם לאלהים
C	Ezek. 36.28	והייתם לי לעם ואנכי אהיה לכם לאליהם
C	Ezek. 37.23	והיו לי לעם ואני אהיה להם לאלהים
C	Ezek. 37.27	והייתי להם לאלהים והמה יהיו לי לעם
C	Zech. 8.8	והיו־לי לעם ואני אהיה להם לאלהים

BIBLIOGRAPHY OF LITERATURE CITED

Publications by the same author are listed chronologically, according to the date of first publication. English translations may therefore appear to be out of order, the relevant date being that of the first German publication, details of which are given in square brackets.

Albertz, R., *A History of Israelite Religion in the Old Testament Period*, trans. J. Bowden, London 1994 [*Religionsgeschichte Israels in alttestamentlicher Zeit*, GAT 8, 2 vols., Göttingen 1992].

Aurelius, E., *Der Fürbitter Israels: Eine Studie zum Mosebild im Alten Testament*, CB.OT 27, Stockholm 1988.

Bach, R., 'Bauen und Pflanzen', in *Studien zur Theologie der alttestamentlichen Überlieferungen: Festschrift G. von Rad*, Neukirchen 1961, 7–32.

Baltzer, K., *The Covenant Formula*, trans. D. E. Green, Philadelphia 1971 [*Das Bundesformular*, WMANT 4, Neukirchen-Vluyn 1964].

Barr, J., 'Some Semantic Notes on the Covenant', in H. Donner, R. Hanbart and R. Smend (eds.), *Beiträge zur alttestamentlichen Theologie: Festschrift W. Zimmerli*, Göttingen 1977, 22–38.

Blum, E., *Die Komposition der Vätergeschichte*, WMANT 57, Neukirchen-Vluyn 1984.

— *Studien zur Komposition des Pentateuch*, BZAW 189, Berlin and New York 1990.

Buber, M., 'Die Erzählung von Sauls Königswahl', *VT* 6 (1956), 113–173.

Crüsemann, F., *The Torah: Theology and Social History of Old Testament Law*, trans. A. Mahnke, Edinburgh 1996 [*Die Tora: Theologie und Sozialgeschichte des alttestamentlichen Gesetzes*, Munich 1992].

Dohmen, C., 'Der Sinaibund als Neuer Bund nach Ex 19–34', in E. Zenger (ed.), *Der Neue Bund im Alten: Zur Bundestheologie der beiden Testamente*, QD 146, Freiburg 1993, 51–83.

Donner, H., *Geschichte des Volkes Israel und seiner Nachbarn in Grundzügen*, GAT 4, vol. 1, Göttingen 1984.

Gamberoni, J., 'קוּם *qûm*', ThWAT 6 (1989), 1252–1274.

Gammie, J. G., *Holiness in Israel*, Minneapolis 1989.

Gaston, L., 'Abraham and the Righteousness of God', *Horizons in Biblical Theology* 2 (1980), 39–68 (reprinted in L. Gaston, *Paul and the Torah*, Vancouver 1987, 45–63).

Greenberg, M., *Ezekiel 1–20*, The Anchor Bible, vol. 22, Garden City, N.Y. 1983.

Gunneweg, A. H. J., *Biblische Theologie des Alten Testaments: Eine Religionsgeschichte Israels in biblisch-theologischer Sicht*, Stuttgart 1993.

Hartley, J. E., *Leviticus*, Word Biblical Commentary, vol. 4, Dallas 1992.

Herrmann, S., 'Die konstruktive Restauration: Das Deuteronomium als Mitte biblischer Theologie', in H. W. Wolff (ed.), *Probleme biblischer Theologie: Festschrift G. von Rad*, Munich 1971, 155–170 (reprinted in S. Herrmann, *Gesammelte Studien zur Geschichte und Theologie des Alten Testaments*, TB 75, Munich 1986, 163–178).

Janowski, B., '"Ich will in eurer Mitte wohnen": Struktur und Genese der exilischen *Schekina*-Theologie', *JBT* 2 (1987), 165–193 (reprinted in B. Janowski, *Gottesgegenwart in Israel*, Neukirchen-Vluyn 1993, 119–147).

Kapelrud, A. S., 'יאל *jᵓl*, TDOT 5, 357–358 [ThWAT 3, 383–384].

Koch, K., *The Growth of the Biblical Tradition: The Form-critical Method*, trans. from the 2nd German edn. by S. M. Cupitt, London and New York 1969 [*Was ist Formgeschichte? Neue Wege der Bibelexegese*, Neukirchen-Vluyn 1964; 5th edn. 1989].

Kutsch, E., *Verheißung und Gesetz*, BZAW 131, Berlin and New York 1973.

Levin, C., *Die Verheißung des Neuen Bundes in ihrem theologiegeschichtlichen Zusammenhang ausgelegt*, FRLANT 137, Göttingen 1985.

Lohfink, N., 'Der Bundesschluß im Land Moab: Redaktionsgeschichtliches zu Dt 28,69–32,47', *BZ NF* 6 (1962), 32–56 (reprinted in *Studien zum Deut.* 1, Stuttgart 1990, 53–82).

— 'Verkündigung des Hauptgebots in der jüngsten Schicht des Deuteronomiums (Dt 4,1–40)', *Bibel und Leben* 5 (1964) (revised version in 'Höre Israel!' (1965), reprinted in *Studien zum Deut.* 1, Stuttgart 1990, 167–191).

— 'Dt 26,17–19 und die "Bundesformel"', *ZKTh* 91 (1969), 517–553 (reprinted in *Studien zum Deut.* 1, Stuttgart 1990, 211–261).

— 'Die Sicherung der Wirksamkeit des Gotteswort durch das Prinzip der Schriftlichkeit der Tora und durch das Prinzip der Gewaltenteilung nach den Ämtergesetzen des Buches Deuteronomium (Dt 16,18–18,22)', in *Testimonium Veritati: Festschrift W. Kempf*, Frankfurt 1971 (reprinted in *Studien zum Deut.* 1, Stuttgart 1990, 305–323).

— 'Die Abänderung der Theologie des priesterlichen Geschichtswerks im Segen des Heiligkeitsgesetzes: Zu Lev. 26,9. 11–13', in *Wort und Geschichte: Festschrift K. Elliger*, Neukirchen-Vluyn 1973, 129–136 (reprinted in *Studien zum Pentateuch*, Stuttgart 1988, 157–168).

— 'Bundestheologie im Alten Testamen: Zum gleichnamigen Buch von Lothar Perlitt', 1973, unpublished (later printed in *Studien zum Deut.* 1, Stuttgart 1990, 325–361).

— *Die Väter Israels im Deuteronomium: Mit einer Stellungnahme von Thomas Römer*, OBO 111, Göttingen 1991.

McEvenue, S. E., *The Narrative Style of the Priestly Writer*, AnBib 50, Rome 1971.

Millard, A. R., 'Abraham', in *Anchor Bible Dictionary*, vol. 1, New York and London 1992, 35–41.

Mosis, R., '"Glauben" und "Gerechtigkeit"—zu Gen 15,6', in *Die Väter Israels: Festschrift J. Schreiner*, Stuttgart 1989, 225–275.

Nicholson, E. W., *God and his People: Covenant and Theology in the Old Testament*, Oxford 1986.

Noth, M., *Überlieferungsgeschichtliche Studien I: Die sammelnden und bearbeitenden Geschichtswerke im Alten Testament*, SKG:G 18.2, Halle and Saale, 1943.

Oeming, M., 'Ist Gen 15,6 ein Beleg für die Anrechnung des Glaubens zur Gerechtigkeit?', *ZAW* 95 (1983), 182–197.

Otto, E., 'Das Heiligkeitsgesetz Leviticus 17–26 in der Pentateuchre-daktion', in *Altes Testament, Forschung und Wirkung: Festschrift H. Graf Reventlow*, Frankfurt etc. 1994.

Perlitt, L., *Bundestheologie im Alten Testament*, WMANT 36, Neukirchen-Vluyn 1969.

von Rad, G., *Das Gottesvolk im Deuteronomium*, BWANT 47, Leipzig 1929.

Rendtorff, R., 'Zum Gebrauch der Formel $n^{e\,\jmath}um$ *jahwe* im Jeremia-buch', *ZAW* 66 (1954), 27–37 (reprinted in *Gesammelte Studien*, Munich 1975, 256–266).

— *Studien zur Geschichte des Opfers im Alten Israel*, WMANT 24, Neukirchen-Vluyn 1967.

— *The Problem of the Process of Transmission in the Pentateuch*, trans. J. J. Scullion, Sheffield 1990 [*Das Überlieferungsgeschichtliche Problem des Pentateuch*, BZAW 147, Berlin and New York 1977].

— *The Old Testament: An Introduction*, trans. John Bowden, London 1985 and Philadelphia 1986 [*Das Alte Testament: Eine Einführung*, Neukirchen-Vluyn 1983; 5th edn. 1995].

— 'Ezekiel 20 and 36.16ff. in the Framework of the Composition of the Book', in R. Rendtorff, *Canon and Theology*, trans. Margaret Kohl, Minneapolis 1993 and Edinburgh 1994, 190–195 ['Ez 20 und 36,16ff im Rahmen der Komposition des Buches Ezechiel', in J. Lust (ed.), *Ezekiel and his Book*, BEThL 74, Gembloux 260–265; also in R. Rendtorff, *Kanon und Theologie*, Neukirchen-Vluyn 1991, 180–184].

— '"Covenant" as a Structuring Concept in Genesis and Exodus', *JBL* 108 (1989), 385–393 (reprinted in Rendtorff, *Canon and Theology*, 125–134; also in Rendtorff, *Kanon und Theologie*, 123–131).

— 'Der Text in seiner Endgestalt: Überlegungen zu Exodus 19', in *Ernten was man sät: Festschrift Klaus Koch*, Neukirchen-Vluyn 1991, 459–470.

— 'Die sündige næfæš', in *Was ist der Mensch ...? Beiträge zur Anthropologie des Alten Testaments: Festschrift H. W. Wolff*, Munich 1992, 211–220.

— 'The Paradigm is Changing: Hopes—and Fears', *Biblical Interpretation* 1 (1993), 34–53.

— ''El als israelitische Gottesbezeichnung. Mit einem Appendix: Beobachtungen zum Gebrauch von האלהים', *ZAW* 106 (1994), 4–21.

Römer, T., *Israels Väter: Untersuchungen zur Väterthematik im Deuteronomium und in der deuteronomistischen Tradition*, OBO 99, Göttingen 1990.

Rotzoll, D. U., 'Gen 15,6—Ein Beleg für den Glauben als Werkgerechtigkeit', *ZAW* 106 (1994), 21–27.

Rudolph, W., *Jeremia*, HAT 12, Tübingen 1958.

Schmid, H. H., 'Ich will euer Gott sein und ihr sollt mein Volk sein: Die sogenannte Bundesformel und die Frage nach der Mitte des Alten Testaments', in *Kirche: Festschrift G. Bornkamm*, Tübingen 1980, 1–25.

Schottroff, W., *'Gedenken' im Alten Orient und im Alten Testament*, WMANT 15, Neukirchen-Vluyn 1963; 2nd edn. 1967.

Ska, J.-L., 'La place d'Ex 6,2–8 dans la narration de l'exode', *ZAW* 94 (1982), 530–548.

— 'Quelques remarques sur P^g et la dernière rédaction du Pentateuque', in A. de Pury (ed.), *La Pentateuque en question*, Geneva 1989, 95–125.

Smend, R., 'Die Bundesformel', ThSt(B) 68 (1963) (reprinted in *Die Mitte des Alten Testaments: Gesammelte Studien* 1, BEvTh 99, Munich 1986, 11–39).

— *Die Entstehung des Alten Testaments*, Stuttgart 1978; 5th edn. 1995.

Stoebe, H. J., *Das erste Buch Samuelis*, KAT 8.1, Gütersloh 1973.

Thiel, W., '*Hēfēr berît*: Zum Bundbrechen im Alten Testament', *VT* 20 (1970), 214–229.

— *Die deuteronomistischen Redaktion von Jeremia 1–25*, WMANT 41, Neukirchen-Vluyn 1973.

— *Die deuteronomistische Redaktion von Jeremia 26–45. Mit einer Gesamtbeurteilung der deuteronomistische Redaktion des Buches Jeremia*, WMANT 52, Neukirchen-Vluyn 1981.

Thompson, T. L., *The Historicity of the Patriarchal Narratives: The Quest for the Historical Abraham*, BZAW 133, Berlin and New York 1974.

Van Seters, J., *Abraham in History and Tradition*, New Haven 1975.

Westermann, C., *Genesis 12–36*, trans. J. J. Scullion, Minneapolis 1985 [*Genesis 12–36*, BK 1/2, Neukirchen-Vluyn 1981].

Zenger, E., 'Die Bundestheologie—ein derzeit vernachlässigtes Thema der Bibelwissenschaft und ein wichtiges Thema für das Verhältnis Israel-Kirche', in *Der Neue Bund im Alten: Zur Bundestheologie der beiden Testamente*, QD 146, Freiburg 1993, 13–49.

Zimmerli, W., 'Das zweite Gebot', in *Festschrift A. Bertholet*, Tübingen 1950, 550–563 (reprinted in W. Zimmerli, *Gottes Offenbarung*, Munich 1963, 234–248).

— 'Ich bin Jahweh', in *Geschichte und Altes Testament: Festschrift A. Alt*, BHTh 16, Tübingen 1953, 179–209 (reprinted in W. Zimmerli, *Gottes Offenbarung*, Munich 1963, 11–40).

— 'Erkenntnis Gottes nach dem Buche Ezechiel', AThANT 27, Zurich 1954 (reprinted in W. Zimmerli, *Gottes Offenbarung*, Munich 1963, 41–119).

— 'Sinaibund und Abrahambund: Ein Beitrag zum Verständnis der Priesterschrift', ThZ 16 (1960), 268–280 (reprinted in W. Zimmerli, *Gottes Offenbarung*, Munich 1963, 205–216).

— *Ezekiel*, trans. R. E. Clements (vol. 1) and J. D. Martin (vol. 2), Hermeneia, Philadelphia 1979, 1983 [*Ezechiel*, BK 13.1, 2, Neukirchen-Vluyn 1969].

INDEX OF NAMES

INDEX OF SELECTED BIBLICAL REFERENCES